NEW

DIRECTIONS

*Five One-Act plays in
the modern idiom*

Edited by

ALAN DURBAND

HUTCHINSON OF LONDON

Hutchinson & Co (Publishers) Ltd
3 Fitzroy Square, London W1

London Melbourne Sydney Auckland
Wellington Johannesburg Cape Town
and agencies throughout the world

First published July 1961
This revised edition May 1975
This selection © Alan Durband 1961

Printed in Great Britain by offset litho by
Flarepath Printers Ltd, St Albans, Herts
and bound by Wm Brendon & Son Ltd
of Tiptree, Essex

ISBN 0 09 061291 4

139217

Acknowledgements

For permission to reprint the plays in this volume the editor is grateful to the following authors and their agents or publishers:

The Representatives of the Dylan Thomas Estate and Messrs J. M. Dent and Sons Ltd for *Return Journey*; the author and Messrs John Calder Ltd for *The Bald Prima Donna*; the author and Messrs Samuel French Ltd for *A Resounding Tinkle*; the author and Miss Margaret Ramsay Ltd for *Barnstable*; the author and Messrs ACTAC (Theatrical and Cinematic) Ltd for *Out of the Flying Pan*.

Contents

Introduction

The ghosts that are said to haunt our older theatres had a miserable ten years after the end of the Second World War. They must have groaned when demolition gangs, Bingo companies, and warehousemen moved in to desecrate the hallowed bricks, mortar and gilded stucco that had for so long been the home of British entertainment. A decline that had begun with the development of cinema was accelerated by the post-war boom in television: between the two, the theatre didn't stand much of a chance.

Small wonder that when NEW DIRECTIONS was first published, the Introduction began with the pessimistic words: 'All over Britain, theatres are closing down'. It really did seem in 1961 that live theatre had had its day – in spite of the fact that five years earlier, in 1956, the astonishing success of John Osborne's LOOK BACK IN ANGER at the Royal Court Theatre, Sloane Square, had heralded a dramatic revolution.

Theatres continued to be victims of property developers and short-sighted local councils. Up and down the country they disappeared, or were put to other uses. Anyone who had proposed the building of a new theatre would have been guaranteed a certificate of lunacy. The Arts Council was operating on a grant even smaller than the subsidy on eggs.

But British theatre, like its ghosts, was only pretending to be dead. It simply refused to lie down. John Osborne had something to say, and a style to say it in, that belonged essentially to the stage. The commercial success of his play enabled the English Stage Company to encourage more young playwrights. The quality and diversity of their work kept the momentum going, and NEW DIRECTIONS was an attempt to represent by means of short plays the vitality and originality of the new movement then beginning to take shape.

Playwrights appeared in great numbers, from all walks of life and all corners of the British Isles: Shelagh Delaney from Salford; Arnold Wesker, Harold Pinter and Bernard Kops from the East End of London; Brendan Behan from Ireland; Henry Livings from Lancashire. It seemed as though a huge reservoir of dramatic talent had burst its banks. The playwright's traditional centre of interest – the middle classes – shifted. The culture, accent, and day-to-day pre-occupations of the working class now provided him with his working material. A new term was coined: 'Kitchen sink drama'. From Europe came the influence of Brecht, who rejected make-believe; his are committed plays, dependent for success on an alert and critical audience. Joan Littlewood, after a lifetime of pioneer experiments in the North, finally settled her Theatre Workshop company at the Theatre Royal, Stratford East. Using Brechtian techniques she converted a new audience to a new style of theatre, at the same time discovering and influencing a number of highly original playwrights.

Twenty years after LOOK BACK IN ANGER, the directions of British theatre are much clearer. The 'Angry Young Man' phase now belongs to history, and without a sign of diminishing energy our playwrights are pushing forward the frontiers of dramatic expression. A survey of our significant contemporary dramatists would be a long one. Robert Bolt, John Mortimer, Tom Stoppard, Ann Jellicoe, John Arden, Alun Owen, Peter Shaffer, David

Mercer, Alan Plater, Charles Dyer, Peter Terson – these are but some of the many gifted writers working today. The astonishing thing is that there are so many others, and that the soil that feeds them is as fertile as ever.

So it isn't surprising – though it certainly is gratifying – to be able to record in this updated version of NEW DIREC-TIONS that all over Britain, theatres are being built. They are appearing in all kinds of shape, size, and overall format, to meet the modern need for flexibility. Nudged along by Arts Associations, and with the help where appropriate of the Arts Council of Great Britain, farsighted towns and cities are subsidising the cultural needs of ratepayers, and once again people are turning to the live theatre for their entertainment. New audiences of young people are being bred, and older theatregoers are being encouraged to sample new styles.

What sort of shock awaits the theatregoer unfamiliar with the new idiom? The five plays that follow offer a clue. The first, RETURN JOURNEY by Dylan Thomas, was written long before the others, and then for radio rather than the stage. But it is a prototype. From it developed UNDER MILK WOOD, a play for voices. Gone is the idea that a well-made play can only be built around the conversations of a few major characters, some supporting ones, a strong plot-line and a realistic set. The modern theatregoer appreciates the role that lighting can play, and the use of contrasting levels and areas of acting. He will enjoy Dylan Thomas's poetic language, and share a journey of discovery rather than sit back and be entertained.

In the case of Ionesco, the shock will be much stronger. THE BALD PRIMA DONNA's one familiar feature is its setting; once the dialogue starts, we are up to our English necks in the Theatre of the Absurd. This satire against the bourgeoisie grew, so the author tells us, from studying idiotic phrases in a French-English conversation book. The commonplace quality of the language brought home to him a simple revelation that communication is composed of threadbare platitudes. The bourgeois develops the secret of talking and saying nothing because, Ionesco believes, he has 'nothing personal to say'. Not such an absurd idea, perhaps, after all.

N. F. Simpson's A RESOUNDING TINKLE belongs to the same school. A shorter version of a prize-winning play, it too is a satire on suburban mediocrity; fans of THE GOON SHOW and MONTY PYTHON'S FLYING CIRCUS will appreciate the humour without having to make many adjustments. BARNSTABLE, however, has an added dimension. James Saunders' play is based on conventional repertory characters in a conventional setting, but this time the idiom is that of the Theatre of Menace. Thrushes fall; roofs collapse: something not defined, but dreadful, is destroying a way of life . . .

In the last play, David Campton's OUT OF THE FLYING PAN, normal communication breaks down completely. In the world of international diplomacy, this is no problem: as George Orwell predicted in *1984*, *Duckspeak* will do just as well. Campton here illustrates one of its most widely-used dialects – the garbled platitude, the scrambled cliché. This inspired piece of clowning demonstrates what has been gained from pointing contemporary theatre in New Directions: it is possible to convey a dramatic message with crystal clarity when the playwright is free to choose his own form and language.

Here, then, are five one-act plays. In the modern idiom.

ALAN DURBAND

1975

Dylan Thomas

Dylan Thomas was born in Swansea ('an ugly, lovely town . . . crawling and sprawling, slummed, unplanned, jerry-villa'd and smug-suburbed') on 27 October 1914. He attended Swansea Grammar School, where his father taught English, and then became a junior reporter on a local newspaper. In 1934 his first volume of poetry was published and he moved to London, where he enjoyed a considerable reputation as a poet and a certain notoriety as a Bohemian. He died in New York on 9 November 1953, at the height of his fame, which he had won as poet, broadcaster, raconteur, poetry-reciter, and, ultimately, dramatist.

Although essentially a poet, it is as a writer of highly individualized prose that he is most widely known and read. Possessed with what he characteristically called 'the lovely gift of the gab', Dylan Thomas poured into his sentences a dazzling variety of compound words, evocative adjectives, alliterations, puns, and verbal contortions. He had the voice to do this prose full justice, a voice with remarkable range and resonance—'speaks rather fancy' says the narrator modestly—and his Broadcast Talks were a feature of the Welsh Home Service for over a dozen years.

Dylan Thomas's development as a dramatist begins with a talk he called *Quite Early One Morning*. This describes the awakening of a Welsh seaside town after a cold and stormy night, and though the script is purely narrative, he peoples it with lifelike characters.

Then comes *Return Journey*, properly described as a 'talks feature', in which autobiography and reminiscence are projected by means of dialogue, with occasional interruptions from the narrator, who is the author himself. Put together the plan and general conception of *Quite Early One Morning*, dramatize it along the lines of *Return Journey*, transfer the narrative to the impersonal First and Second Voices, and you have *Under Milk Wood*. Though it was originally commissioned for radio, this play was a signal success in the theatre, where it gave fresh hope for the future of poetic drama when it had its world première at the Edinburgh Festival in 1956.

Return Journey speaks for itself, or rather, Dylan Thomas. The description of the shopping women in the narrator's opening speech is characteristic of his prose; the description of Young Thomas ('above medium height for Wales, I mean, he's five foot six and a half') is typical of his wit; the interplay of voices as they fade in and out, like memories, is representative of his method in the full-scale *Under Milk Wood*.

The irony of the play's last lines is that of fate.

Eugene Ionesco

Eugene Ionesco is Europe's most controversial playwright. Born in Bucharest, Rumania, in 1912, he spent his early years in France and returned there at the age of twenty-seven to work for a publishing house. He is now a naturalized French subject.

Success did not come easily to him. His early works were rejected by publishers and theatre managers, and it was not until 1950 that he was able to see his first play, *The Bald Prima Donna*, produced at a tiny off-beat theatre in Paris. Two of the three critics present called it 'dull and worthless' but his second play, *The Lesson*, produced in 1951, was received with some enthusiasm by the younger critics. By the time *The Chairs* appeared in 1952, the tide had turned. Samuel Beckett, the author of *Waiting for Godot*, praised him; and Jean Anouilh said he preferred Ionesco's plays to those of Strindberg.

By 1958 Ionesco was, in his own words, 'a dumbfounded success' in Paris, London, and New York. His works have been produced in Italy, Germany, Israel, Switzerland, Poland, Yugoslavia, and Brazil. A double bill consisting of *The Bald Prima Donna* and *The Lesson* opened in Paris in 1957 and was still running in 1960.

The plays of Ionesco are indisputably a challenge. Critics and audiences have reacted violently to them. When his *Jacques* was first produced in 1955, fights broke out in the foyer because the hero chooses a girl with three noses as his fiancée. Disturbances are no unusual thing in the theatre when a playwright challenges established conventions— Goldsmith's *She Stoops to Conquer* was booed and hissed on its first night, and J. M. Synge narrowly avoided a lynching when *The Playboy of the Western World* was first produced at the Abbey Theatre, Dublin. Nothing would be easier than to dismiss as sheer nonsense the banality of Ionesco's situations and the surrealism of his humour. Those who can resist the temptation may well go on to share the growing feeling amongst critics that beneath the eccentric exterior lies a significant philosophy.

It is not simply that Ionesco's text is the futility or impossibility of communication, although this is well illustrated in his plays; it is far more disturbing than that. 'The human drama,' Ionesco has said, 'is as absurd as it is painful.' Comedy and tragedy are to him merely aspects of the same situation, so that the unbearable predicament often erupts into pure farce.

Deliberately, Ionesco chooses to write plays about nothing, rather than what he calls the secondary problems of society and politics. Obsessed as he is with the emptiness and frustration of this world, he relies more upon the failure of his characters to engage with each other than with plot and the interplay of personalities. Irrelevance is intentional, and the clichés and inanities of common speech which predominate in his dialogue are all seen to be central to his purpose, which is to stress 'a hollow automation' and 'a spiritual rootlessness' which pervade contemporary civilization.

'In all my plays,' says Ionesco, 'I try to present a critique of some form of conformist thought and phoney verbiage.' After you have read *The Bald Prima Donna* you may or may not agree that he has succeeded in his purpose. But one thing is sure: you will not easily forget the experience of reading him.

Of how many playwrights in the conventional theatre could you say the same?

N. F. Simpson

A Londoner 'by birth and inclination', N. F. Simpson spent a couple of years in a bank before the war (during which he was in the Intelligence Corps), but afterwards took up teaching. In spite of his success as a playwright he has not quitted the classroom.

Mr Simpson first won recognition as a dramatist with a full-length version of *A Resounding Tinkle*, which won third prize in the *Observer* Play Competition. In a slightly reshaped form it was produced by the English Stage Company at the Royal Court Theatre, Sloane Square, as a Production-Without-Décor. Eventually the play was condensed to its present length. His second full-length play *One Way Pendulum* was produced at the same theatre.

N. F. Simpson's plays are hilarious exercises of wit in which the commonplace activities of life are wildly distorted, in such a gravely serious way that his characters never sense the insanity themselves. To them, everything is of consequence, everything is normal, everything is properly proportioned. Nothing could be more ordinary than the Paradocks' suburban home, or for that matter the Paradocks themselves—until they start talking. The same deadpan seriousness is in *One Way Pendulum*, which provides, according to the theatre programme, 'an evening of high drung and slarrit'. Patrons were set off on the right foot with a selection of typical Simpson inanities:

> 'Friends and survivors. I should like, if I may for a brief moment, to speak up among the gamma rays here, for the traditional disciplines and age-old ways of thought but for which total extinction might have been no more than the pipe-dream of some mad visionary.'

'A good egg is an egg-shaped egg. Once an egg begins to break with its true shape, it is only a matter of time before it acquires wings and feathers. And along that road, make no mistake about it, lie the flying egg, the mating egg, and—ultimate absurdity—the egg-laying egg.'

As for *A Resounding Tinkle*, if it needs any justification at all, let this, Mr Simpson's own apologia, be reason enough:

'They say that, cataclysms apart, there are another twelve hundred thousand million years ahead of us all yet. These will have to be got through somehow, preferably without fuss, and we must just try and keep ourselves occupied as best we may. It isn't difficult. One can poke things. One can pick things up. Or one can distinguish between one thing and another; or between one group of things and another large group. (Or between several smaller groups.) One can decide whether to decide or whether to leave it to someone else to decide; and there are trigonometry, copulation, travel, counter-espionage— to name but a few of the innumerable activities, from giving massage to the exercise of magnanimity—which compete for those brief moments of leisure when we are not translating poems, torturing people, timing eggs, weeping for the past, heating glue, designing practical joke sets. Or sleeping. Or whistling. Or fighting, each according to his bent: some for freedom, some for the suppression of freedom. There are logs to be chopped, treaties to be signed, people to be snubbed. And there's moving about: how often do we stop to think of all the different speeds we can choose from to move about at? And in other ways, too, we can diversify our lives. If we try.'

James Saunders

James Saunders was born in Islington, London, in 1925. He began his career as a teacher of Chemistry, but while studying for a degree at Southampton he discovered an interest in writing dialogue, and this has been an obsession with him ever since. He is the author of a number of plays for radio, but his best known work is for the theatre and television: NEXT TIME I'LL SING TO YOU, A SCENT OF FLOWERS, THE TRAVAILS OF SANCHO PANZA, THE ITALIAN GIRL (with Iris Murdoch, from her novel), AFTER LIVERPOOL, and a distinguished collection of adaptations from the works of D. H. Lawrence, H. E. Bates, and A. E. Coppard.

Barnstable is the second play in the trilogy *Ends and Echoes* which was produced at the Questors Theatre in 1960. Whereas in David Campton's *Out of the Flying Pan* nuclear warfare is the direct consequence of the ineptitude and folly of diplomacy, and the horror of war is made explicit in the sound effects, in *Barnstable* nuclear destruction is deliberately made remote. Apathy, indifference, and a refusal to face facts: these are what give the play, with its mysterious character Barnstable, a further dimension.

At first sight, *Barnstable* is just another potboiler for Women's Institutes and Village Dramatic Societies, smug with upper-middle-class concern for the garden, and with conventional recourse to telephone calls, flower arrangements, and vacuous maidservants. One by one these postures are debunked. Moles in the lawn are preposterously more important than the collapsing of the west wing and the upper storeys of the house. Helen's self-recrimination comes to an absurd head in her dilemma over Harold's invitation to go riding. A sensitive girl, but one who is inextricably involved in social conformity, she can tell that 'something absolutely inane and dreadful is going to happen'. She cannot escape, though she tries to emigrate. She gets no help from her family or the Church. Carboy, the Imperturbable Robinson of the trenches in 1915, calls for 'a balanced judgment in the light of an all-round assessment of the situation', and Wandsworth Teeter's metaphysics tell him that 'all is as it should be. To be otherwise is impossible.' Sandra, hopelessly out of her depth but ignorant enough to be talked out of her discomfort, drinks her cocoa, pathetically reassured by the reactionary forces which her betters represent. They were not disturbed by Helen's prophecy of doom and they are not affected by her death. Of the survivors, only Daphne knows that Barnstable exists, but she isn't likely to shake off the habits of a lifetime and rise above arranging flowers and preparing cocoa.

In *Barnstable* James Saunders has approached a highly relevant contemporary theme with a perceptive wit and a challenging technique that is all his own, notwithstanding the influence of Ionesco that lies behind some of his dialogue. *The Bald Prima Donna* ends where it begins; the cycle of futility seemingly has no proper climax. In *Barnstable* we are left wondering whether the human race will ever come to terms with the mysterious forces we are compelled to live with in this nuclear age.

Deliberately, the format of James Saunders' play is that of an outmoded style of theatre, and Barnstable, though he never appears, is the most menacingly real of all the characters.

David Campton

David Campton was born over a barber's shop in the back streets of Leicester in 1924. After a false start as a clerk, and an interlude with the R.A.F. as a flight mechanic, he found his true vocation as a writer, both for television and the theatre. While under contract with Associated Rediffusion, he wrote light entertainment sketches, children's programmes, serials, and a number of thrillers. Then for six years he was a member of the late Stephen Joseph's Theatre-in-the-Round company, which staged at least one of his plays each season. The most significant were THE LUNATIC VIEW and A VIEW FROM THE BRINK – both concerned with mankind's unique situation in the twentieth century as a consequence of nuclear weapons. His output since then has been prolific, and besides writing plays, he still finds some time to act in them. His most recent successes are THE LIFE AND DEATH OF ALMOST EVERYBODY, and his adaptation of FRANKENSTEIN. His play THE RIGHT PLACE is in the Hutchinson PLAYBILL ONE collection, and is further evidence of the author's strong moral commitment. OUT OF THE FLYING PAN is a biting satire on international diplomacy; words break down, but the message is clear, though grim.

No-one could accuse contemporary theatre of complacency.

Return Journey

by

DYLAN THOMAS

First Broadcast 15 June 1947 on the
B.B.C. Home Service. Producer, P. H. Burton

Cast

NARRATOR
BARMAID
CUSTOMER
FIRST VOICE
SECOND VOICE
THIRD VOICE
FOURTH VOICE
OLD REPORTER
FIRST YOUNG REPORTER
SECOND YOUNG REPORTER
PASSER-BY
SCHOOLMASTER
VOICE
PROMENADE-MAN
GIRL
PARK-KEEPER

Return Journey

NARRATOR: It was a cold white day in High Street, and
nothing to stop the wind slicing up from the docks, for
where the squat and tall shops had shielded the town from
the sea lay their blitzed flat graves marbled with snow and
headstoned with fences. Dogs, delicate as cats on water,
as though they had gloves on their paws, padded over the
vanished buildings. Boys romped, calling high and clear,
on top of a levelled chemist's and a shoe-shop, and a little
girl, wearing a man's cap, threw a snowball in a chill
deserted garden that had once been the Jug and Bottle of
the Prince of Wales. The wind cut up the street with a
soft sea-noise hanging on its arm, like a hooter in a muffler.
I could see the swathed hill stepping up out of the town,
which you never could see properly before, and the
powdered fields of the roofs of Milton Terrace and Watkin
Street, and Fullers Row. Fish-frailed, netbagged, umbrella'd,
pixie-capped, fur-shoed, blue-nosed, puce-lipped, blinkered
like drayhorses, scarved, mittened, galoshed, wearing
everything but the cat's blanket, crushes of shopping-
women crunched in the little Lapland of the once grey
drab street, blew and queued and yearned for hot tea, as I
began my search through Swansea town cold and early on
that wicked February morning. I went into the hotel.
'Good morning.'

The hall-porter did not answer. I was just another snow-
man to him. He did not know that I was looking for

someone after fourteen years, and he did not care. He stood and shuddered, staring through the glass of the hotel door at the snowflakes sailing down the sky, like Siberian confetti. The bar was just opening, but already one customer puffed and shook at the counter with a full pint of half-frozen Tawe water in his wrapped-up hand. I said Good morning, and the barmaid, polishing the counter vigorously as though it were a rare and valuable piece of Swansea china, said to her first customer:

BARMAID: Seen the film at the Elysium Mr Griffiths there's snow isn't it did you come up on your bicycle our pipes burst Monday . . .

NARRATOR: A pint of bitter, please.

BARMAID: Proper little lake in the kitchen got to wear your Wellingtons when you boil a egg one and four please . . .

CUSTOMER: The cold gets me just here . . .

BARMAID: . . . and eightpence change that's your liver Mr Griffiths you been on the cocoa again . . .

NARRATOR: I wonder whether you remember a friend of mine? He always used to come to this bar, some years ago. Every morning, about this time.

CUSTOMER: Just by here it gets me. I don't know what'd happen if I didn't wear a band . . .

BARMAID: What's his name?

NARRATOR: Young Thomas.

BARMAID: Lots of Thomases come here it's a kind of home from home for Thomases isn't it Mr Griffiths what's he look like?

NARRATOR: He'd be about seventeen or eighteen . . . [*Slowly*]

BARMAID: . . . I was seventeen once . . .

NARRATOR: . . . and above medium height. Above medium height for Wales, I mean, he's five foot six and a half. Thick blubber lips; snub nose; curly mousebrown hair; one front tooth broken after playing a game called Cats and Dogs, in the Mermaid, Mumbles; speaks rather fancy; truculent; plausible; a bit of a shower-off; plus-fours and no breakfast, you know; used to have poems printed in the *Herald of Wales*; there was one about an open-air performance of *Electra* in Mrs Bertie Perkins's garden in Sketty; lived up the Uplands; a bombastic adolescent provincial Bohemian with a thick-knotted artist's tie made out of his sister's scarf, she never knew where it had gone, and a cricket-shirt dyed bottle-green; a gabbing, ambitious, mock-tough, pretentious young man; and mole-y, too.

BARMAID: There's words what d'you want to find *him* for I wouldn't touch him with a barge-pole . . . would you, Mr Griffiths? Mind, you can never tell. I remember a man came here with a monkey. Called for 'alf for himself and a pint for the monkey. And he wasn't Italian at all. Spoke Welsh like a preacher.

NARRATOR: The bar was filling up. Snowy business bellies pressed their watch-chains against the counter; black business bowlers, damp and white now as Christmas puddings in their cloths, bobbed in front of the misty mirrors. The voice of commerce rang sternly through the lounge.

FIRST VOICE: Cold enough for you?

SECOND VOICE: How's your pipes, Mr Lewis?

THIRD VOICE: Another winter like this'll put paid to me, Mr Evans.

FOURTH VOICE: I got the 'flu . . .

FIRST VOICE: Make it a double . . .

SECOND VOICE: Similar . . .

BARMAID: Okay, baby . . .

CUSTOMER: I seem to remember a chap like you described. There couldn't be two like him let's hope. He used to work as a reporter. Down the Three Lamps I used to see· him. Lifting his ikkle elbow. [*Confidentially*]

NARRATOR: What's the Three Lamps like now?

CUSTOMER: It isn't like anything. It isn't there. It's nothing mun. You remember Ben Evans's stores? It's right next door to that. Ben Evans isn't there either . . . [Fade]

NARRATOR: I went out of the hotel into the snow and walked down High Street, past the flat white wastes where all the shops had been. Eddershaw Furnishers, Curry's Bicycles, Donegal Clothing Company, Doctor Scholl's, Burton Tailors, W. H. Smith, Boots Cash Chemists, Leslie's Stores, Upson's Shoes, Prince of Wales, Tucker's Fish, Stead & Simpson—all the shops bombed and vanished. Past the hole in space where Hodges & Clothiers had been, down Castle Street, past the remembered invisible shops, Price's Fifty Shilling, and Crouch the Jeweller, Potter Gilmore Gowns, Evans Jeweller, Master's Outfitters, Style and Mantle, Lennard's Boots, True Form, Kardomah, R. E. Jones, Dean's Tailor, David Evans, Gregory Confectioners, Bovega, Burton's, Lloyd's Bank, and nothing. And into Temple Street. There the Three Lamps had stood, old Mac magisterial in his corner. And there the Young Thomas whom I was searching for used to stand at the counter on Friday paynights with Freddie Farr Half Hook, Bill Latham, Cliff Williams, Gareth Hughes, Eric Hughes, Glyn Lowry, a man among men, his hat at a rakish angle, in that snug, smug, select, Edwardian holy of best-bitter holies . . . [Bar noises in background]

OLD REPORTER: Remember when I took you down the mortuary for the first time, Young Thomas? He'd never seen a corpse before, boys, except old Ron on a Saturday night. 'If you want to be a proper newspaperman,' I said, 'you got to be well known in the right circles. You got to be *persona grata* in the mortuary, see.' He went pale green, mun.

FIRST YOUNG REPORTER: Look, he's blushing now . . .

OLD REPORTER: And when we got there what d'you think? The decorators were in at the mortuary, giving the old home a bit of a re-do like. Up on ladders having a slap at the roof. Young Thomas didn't see 'em, he had his pop eyes glued on the slab, and when one of the painters up the ladder said 'Good morning, gents' in a deep voice he upped in the air and out of the place like a ferret. Laugh!

BARMAID [off]: You've had enough, Mr Roberts.

You heard what I said. [Noise of a gentle scuffle]

SECOND YOUNG REPORTER [casually]: There goes Mr Roberts.

OLD REPORTER: Well fair do's they throw you out very genteel in this pub . . .

FIRST YOUNG REPORTER: Ever seen Young Thomas covering a soccer match down the Vetch and working it out in tries?

SECOND YOUNG REPORTER: And up the Mannesman Hall shouting 'Good footwork, sir,' and a couple of punch-drunk colliers galumphing about like jumbos.

FIRST YOUNG REPORTER: What you been reporting today, Young Thomas?

SECOND YOUNG REPORTER: Two typewriter Thomas the ace news-dick . . .

OLD REPORTER: Let's have a dekko at your note-book. 'Called at British Legion: Nothing. Called at Hospital: One broken leg. Auction at the Metropole. Ring Mr Beynon *re* Gymanfa Ganu. Lunch: Pint and pasty at the Singleton with Mrs Giles. Bazaar at Bethesda Chapel. Chimney on fire at Tontine Street. Walters Road Sunday School Outing. Rehearsal of the *Mikado* at Skewen'—all front page stuff . . . [Fade]

NARRATOR: The voices of fourteen years ago hung silent in the snow and ruin, and in the falling winter morning I walked on through the white havoc'd centre where once a very young man I knew had mucked about as chirpy as a sparrow after the sips and titbits and small change of the town. Near the *Evening Post* building and the fragment of the Castle I stopped a man whose face I thought I recognized from a long time ago. I said: I wonder if you can tell me . . .

PASSER-BY: Yes?

NARRATOR: He peered out of his blanketing scarves and from under his snowballed Balaclava like an Eskimo with a bad conscience. I said: If you can tell me whether you used to know a chap called Young Thomas. He worked on the *Post* and used to wear an overcoat sometimes with the check lining inside out so that you could play giant draughts on him. He wore a conscious woodbine, too . . .

PASSER-BY: What d'you mean, conscious woodbine?

NARRATOR: . . . and a perched pork pie with a peacock feather and he tried to slouch like a newshawk even when he was attending a meeting of the Gorseinon Buffalos . . .

PASSER-BY: Oh, *him*! He owes me half a crown. I haven't seen him since the old Kardomah days. He wasn't a reporter then, he'd just left the grammar school. Him and Charlie Fisher—Charlie's got whiskers now—and Tom Warner and Fred Janes, drinking coffee-dashes and arguing the toss.

NARRATOR: What about?

PASSER-BY: Music and poetry and painting and politics. Einstein and Epstein, Stravinsky and Greta Garbo, death and religion, Picasso and girls . . .

NARRATOR: And then?

PASSER-BY: Communism, symbolism, Bradman, Braque, the Watch Committee, free love, free beer, murder, Michelangelo, ping-pong, ambition, Sibelius, and girls . . .

NARRATOR: Is that all?

PASSER-BY: How Dan Jones was going to compose the most

prodigious symphony, Fred Janes paint the most miraculously meticulous picture, Charlie Fisher catch the poshest trout, Vernon Watkins and Young Thomas write the most boiling poems, how they would ring the bells of London and paint it like a tart . . .

NARRATOR: And after that?

PASSER-BY: Oh the hissing of the butt-ends in the drains of the coffee-dashes and the tinkle and the gibble-gabble of the morning young lounge lizards as they talked about Augustus John, Emil Jannings, Carnera, Dracula, Amy Johnson, trial marriage, pocket-money, the Welsh sea, the London stars, King Kong, anarchy, darts, T. S. Eliot, and girls. . . . Duw, it's cold!

NARRATOR: And he hurried on, into the dervish snow, without a good morning or good-bye, swaddled in his winter woollens like a man in the island of his deafness, and I felt that perhaps he had never stopped at all to tell me of one more departed stage in the progress of the boy I was pursuing. The Kardomah Café was razed to the snow, the voices of the coffee-drinkers—poets, painters, and musicians in their beginnings—lost in the willynilly flying of the years and the flakes.

Down College Street I walked then, past the remembered invisible shops, Langley's, Castle Cigar Co., T. B. Brown, Pullar's, Aubrey Jeremiah, Goddard Jones, Richards, Hornes, Marles, Pleasance & Harper, Star Supply, Sidney Heath, Wesley Chapel, and nothing. . . . My search was leading me back, through pub and job and café, to the School. [*Fade*] [*School bell*]

SCHOOLMASTER: Oh yes, yes, I remember him well,
though I do not know if I would recognize him now:
nobody grows any younger, or better,
and boys grow into much the sort of men one would
suppose
though sometimes the moustaches bewilder

31

and one finds it hard to reconcile one's memory of a small
none-too-clean urchin lying his way unsuccessfully out
of his homework
with a fierce and many-medalled sergeant-major with
three children or a divorced chartered accountant;
and it is hard to realize
that some little tousled rebellious youth whose only
claim
to fame among his contemporaries was his undisputed
right
to the championship of the spitting contest
is now perhaps one's own bank manager.
Oh yes, I remember him well, the boy you are searching
for:
he looked like most boys, no better, brighter, or more
respectful;
he cribbed, mitched, spilt ink, rattled his desk and
garbled his lessons with the worst of them;
he could smudge, hedge, smirk, wriggle, wince,
whimper, blarney, badger, blush, deceive, be
devious, stammer, improvise, assume
offended dignity or righteous indignation as though to
the manner born;
sullenly and reluctantly he drilled, for some small
crime, under Sergeant Bird, so wittily nicknamed
Oiseau, on Wednesday half-holidays,
appeared regularly in detention classes,
hid in the cloakroom during algebra,
was, when a newcomer, thrown into the bushes of the
Lower Playground by bigger boys,
and threw newcomers into the bushes of the Lower
Playground when *he* was a bigger boy;
he scuffled at prayers,
he interpolated, smugly, the time-honoured wrong
irreverent words into the morning hymns,

he helped to damage the headmaster's rhubarb,
was thirty-third in trigonometry,
and, as might be expected, edited the School Magazine.

[*Fade*]

NARRATOR: The Hall is shattered, the echoing corridors charred where he scribbled and smudged and yawned in the long green days, waiting for the bell and the scamper into the Yard: the School on Mount Pleasant Hill has changed its face and its ways. Soon, they say, it may be no longer the School at all he knew and loved when he was a boy up to no good but the beat of his blood: the names are havoc'd from the Hall and the carved initials burned from the broken wood. But the names remain. What names did he know of the dead? Who of the honoured dead did he know such a long time ago? The names of the dead in the living heart and head remain for ever. Of all the dead whom did he know? [*Funeral bell*]

VOICE:

Evans, K. J.
Haines, G. C.
Roberts, I. L.
Moxham, J.
Thomas, H.
Baines, W.
Bazzard, F. H.
Beer, L. J.
Bucknell, R.
Tywford, G.
Vagg, E. A.
Wright, G. [*Fade*]

NARRATOR: Then I tacked down the snowblind hill, a cat-o'-nine-gales whipping from the sea, and, white and eider-downed in the smothering flurry, people padded past me up and down like prowling featherbeds. And I plodded through the ankle-high one cloud that foamed the town, into flat Gower Street, its buildings melted, and along long Helen's Road. Now my search was leading me back to the seashore. [*Noise of sea, softly*]

NARRATOR: Only two living creatures stood on the promenade, near the cenotaph, facing the tossed crystal sea: a man in a chewed muffler and a ratting cap, and an angry dog of a mixed make. The man dithered in the cold, beat his bare blue hands together, waited for some sign from sea or snow; the dog shouted at the weather, and fixed his bloodshot eyes on Mumbles Head. But when the man and I talked together, the dog piped down and fixed his eyes on me, blaming me for the snow. The man spoke towards the sea. Year in, year out, whatever the weather, once in the daytime, in the dark, he always came to look at the sea. He knew all the dogs and boys and old men who came to see the sea, who ran or gambolled on the sand or stooped at the edge of the waves as though over a wild, wide, rolling ash-can. He knew the lovers who went to lie in the sandhills, the striding masculine women who roared at their terriers like tiger tamers, the loafing men whose work it was in the world to observe the great employment of the sea. He said:

PROMENADE-MAN: Oh yes, yes, I remember him well, but I didn't know what was his name. I don't know the names of none of the sandboys. They don't know mine. About fourteen or fifteen years old, you said, with a little red cap. And he used to play by Vivian's Stream. He used to dawdle in the arches, you said, and lark about on the railway-lines and holler at the old sea. He'd mooch about the dunes and watch the tankers and the tugs and the banana boats come out of the docks. He was going to run away to sea, he said. *I* know. On Saturday afternoon he'd go down to the sea when it was a long way out, and hear the foghorns though he couldn't see the ships. And on Sunday nights, after chapel, he'd be swaggering with his pals along the prom, whistling after the girls. [*Titter*]

GIRL: Does your mother know you're out? Go away now. Stop following us. [*Another girl titters*]

GIRL: Don't you say nothing, Hetty, you're only encouraging. No thank *you*, Mr Cheeky, with your cut-glass accent and your father's trilby! I don't want *no* walk on *no* sands. What d'you say? Ooh listen to him, Het, he's swallowed a dictionary. No, I don't want to go with nobody up no lane in the moonlight, see, and I'm not a baby-snatcher neither. I seen you going to school along Terrace Road, Mr Glad-Eye, with your little satchel and wearing your red cap and all. You seen me wearing my . . . no you never. Hetty, mind your glasses! Hetty Harris, you're as bad as them. Oh go away and do your homework, you. No I'm not then. I'm nobody's homework, see. Cheek! Hetty Harris, don't you let him! Oooh, there's brazen! Well, just to the end of the prom, if you like. No further, mind . . .

PROMENADE-MAN: Oh yes, I knew him well. I've known him by the thousands . . .

NARRATOR: Even now, on the frozen foreshore, a high, far cry of boys, all like the boy I sought, slid on the glass of the streams and snowballed each other and the sky. Then I went on my way from the sea, up Brynmill Terrace and into Glanbrydan Avenue where Bert Trick had kept a grocer's shop and, in the kitchen, threatened the annihilation of the ruling classes over sandwiches and jelly and blancmange. And I came to the shops and houses of the Uplands. Here and around here it was that the journey had begun of the one I was pursuing through his past.

[*Old piano cinema-music in background*]

FIRST VOICE: Here was once the flea-pit picture-house where he whooped for the scalping Indians with Jack Basset and banged for the rustlers' guns.

NARRATOR: Jackie Basset, killed.

THIRD VOICE: Here once was Mrs Ferguson's, who sold the best gob-stoppers and penny packets full of surprises and a sweet kind of glue.

FIRST VOICE: In the fields behind Cwmdonkin Drive, the Murrays chased him and all cats.

SECOND VOICE: No fires now where the outlaws' fires burned and the paradisiacal potatoes roasted in the embers.

THIRD VOICE: In the Graig beneath Town Hill he was a lonely killer hunting the wolves (or rabbits) and the red Sioux tribe (or Mitchell brothers).

[*Fade cinema-music into background of children's voices reciting, in unison, the names of the counties of Wales*]

FIRST VOICE: In Mirador School he learned to read and count. Who made the worst raffia doilies? Who put water in Joyce's galoshes, every morning prompt as prompt? In the afternoons, when the children were good, they read aloud from Struwelpeter. And when they were bad, they sat alone in the empty classroom, hearing, from above them, the distant, terrible, sad music of the late piano lesson.

[*The children's voices fade. The piano lesson continues in background*]

NARRATOR: And I went up, through the white Grove, into Cwmdonkin Park, the snow still sailing and the childish, lonely, remembered music fingering on in the suddenly gentle wind. Dusk was folding the Park around, like another, darker snow. Soon the bell would ring for the closing of the gates, though the Park was empty. The park-keeper walked by the reservoir, where swans had glided, on his white rounds. I walked by his side and asked him my questions, up the swathed drives past buried beds and loaded utterly still furred and birdless trees towards the last gate. He said:

PARK-KEEPER: Oh yes, yes, I knew him well. He used to climb the reservoir railings and pelt the old swans. Run like a billygoat over the grass you should keep off of. Cut branches off the trees. Carve words on the benches. Pull up moss in the rockery, go snip through the dahlias. Fight in the bandstand. Climb the elms and moon up the top like a owl. Light fires in the bushes. Play on the green bank. Oh yes, I knew him well. I think he was happy all the time. I've known him by the thousands.

NARRATOR: We had reached the last gate. Dusk drew around us and the town. I said: What has become of him now?

PARK-KEEPER: Dead.

NARRATOR: The Park-keeper said: [*The park bell rings*]

PARK-KEEPER: Dead ... Dead ... Dead ... Dead ... Dead ... Dead.

The Bald Prima Donna

AN ANTI-PLAY

by

EUGENE IONESCO
(*Translated by Donald Watson*)

First produced in Paris by Nicholas Bataille
at the Théâtre des Noctambules, 11 May 1950

First performed in London at the Arts Theatre Club,
6 November 1956. Producer, Peter Wood

Cast

MR SMITH
MRS SMITH
MR MARTIN
MRS MARTIN
THE CAPTAIN OF THE FIRE BRIGADE
THE MAID

The Bald Prima Donna

SCENE: *A typical middle-class English interior. Comfortable arm-chairs. Typical English evening at home. Typical English* MR SMITH, *in his favourite armchair, wearing English slippers, smoking an English pipe, reading an English newspaper, beside an English fire. He is wearing English spectacles, has a small grey English moustache. Next to him, in her favourite armchair, typically English* MRS SMITH *is darning English socks. A long English silence. An English clock chimes three English chimes.*

MRS SMITH: Goodness! Nine o'clock! This evening for supper we had soup, fish, cold ham and mashed potatoes and a good English salad, and we had English beer to drink. The children drank English water. We had a very good meal this evening. And that's because we are English, because we live in a suburb of London and because our name is Smith.

[MR SMITH *goes on reading his newspaper and clicks his tongue*]

Mashed potatoes are very nice with cold ham. The mayonnaise was quite fresh. The mayonnaise from the grocer round the corner is much better quality than the mayonnaise from the grocer opposite, it's even better than the mayonnaise from the grocer at the bottom of the hill. Of course I don't mean to say that his mayonnaise is bad . . .

[MR SMITH, *still reading, clicks his tongue*]

Yet the fact remains that the mayonnaise from the grocer round the corner is the best . . .

[MR SMITH, *still reading, clicks his tongue*]

Mary did the potatoes very well for once. Last time she didn't do them at all well. I only like them when they're done nicely.

[MR SMITH, *still reading, clicks his tongue*]

The fish was nice and fresh. It makes my mouth water to think of it. I took two helpings. No, three! And it always gives me the collywobbles. *You* took three helpings, too. But the third time you took less than the first two times, and *I* took a lot more. I had more to eat than you did this evening. How did that come about? You don't usually suffer from lack of appetite.

[MR SMITH, *still reading, clicks his tongue*]

Our little boy did so want to drink some beer tonight; he'll be fond of a glass or two, when he's older; he takes after you, dear. Did you see him at table, how he couldn't take his eyes off the bottle? But I picked up the jug and poured him out a glass of water. He drank it because he was thirsty. Helen takes after me: she's a good little housewife, very economical and she plays the piano. She never asks to be allowed to drink English beer. Neither does our youngest little girl, who lives on bread and milk. Anyone can tell she's only two years old. Her name is Peggy. The elderberry tart was excellent. Perhaps with the dessert we should have had a little glass of Australian Burgundy, but I didn't put the wine on the table, so as not to set the children a bad example. We must bring them up not to be wild and extravagant.

[MR SMITH, *still reading, clicks his tongue*]

Mrs Parker goes to a Rumanian grocer called Popesco-Rosenfeld, who's just arrived from Constantinople. He's a specialist in yoghourt. He holds a diploma from a school for yoghourticians in Andrinopolis. I think I'll pay him a visit tomorrow and buy a great big pot of real home-made Rumanian yoghourt. It's not often one gets the chance of finding such things here in the suburbs of London.

[MR SMITH, *still reading, clicks his tongue*]

Yoghourt is very good for the stomach, the lumbar regions, appendicitis and apotheosis. At least, that's what Dr Mackenzie-King told me, you know, the one who looks after the Johns' children, the people next door. He's a fine doctor. One can always have faith in what he tells you. He never prescribes anything he hasn't first tried out on himself. Before he made Parker go through that operation last year, he had himself operated on, for liver, you know, although there was nothing wrong with him at the time.

MR SMITH: Then how was it that the Doctor came through it all right and poor old Parker died?

MRS SMITH: Why? Because the operation was successful on the Doctor, and on Parker it wasn't.

MR SMITH: In that case, then, Mackenzie's not a good doctor. Either the operation should have been successful on both of them, or both of them should have gone under.

MRS SMITH: What do you mean?

MR SMITH: Well, if they can't both be cured, a really conscientious doctor ought to die with his patient. The captain goes down with his ship. He doesn't survive the wreck!

MRS SMITH: You can't compare a patient to a boat.

MR SMITH: And why not, pray? After all, even a boat has its little ailments; besides, your doctor's a healthy enough vessel; all the more reason why he should perish at the same time as his patient, like the captain and his ship.

Mrs Smith: Ah! I hadn't thought of that! . . . Perhaps you're right . . . What do you make of it all, then?

Mr Smith: It's very simple. All doctors are charlatans. And all their patients too. The only respectable thing left in England is the Royal Navy.

Mrs Smith: But not sailors.

Mr Smith: No, of course not! [*Still looking at his paper*] There's a thing I can never understand. In the births, deaths and marriages column of the paper, why the devil do they always give the age of the deceased persons and never tell you how old the babies are? It doesn't make sense.

Mrs Smith: It's never struck me before.

> [*The clock strikes seven times. Silence.*
> *The clock strikes three times. Silence.*
> *The clock strikes no times*]

Mr Smith [*still with his paper*]: Well, well, well! According to this, Bobby Watson's dead.

Mrs Smith: Good Heavens! Poor fellow! When did it happen?

Mr Smith: What are you looking so surprised about? You knew perfectly well he was dead. He died about two years ago. You remember, we went to the funeral, about eighteen months ago, it must be.

Mrs Smith: Of course, I remember perfectly. It came back to me at once; but I fail to understand why you had to look so surprised to see it in the paper.

Mr Smith: It wasn't in the paper! It must be three years ago now since there was talk of his passing away. I was reminded of it by an association of ideas.

Mrs Smith: What a shame it was! He was so very well preserved.

Mr Smith: He made the best-looking corpse in Great Britain! And he never looked his age. Poor old Bobby! He'd been dead for four years and he was still warm. A living corpse if ever there was one. And how cheerful he always was!

Mrs Smith: Little Bobby, poor darling!

Mr Smith: What do you mean, 'Poor darling'?

Mrs Smith: I was thinking about his wife. Her name was Bobby, like his. As they had the same name, when you saw them together, you could never tell one from the other. It was really only after he died that you could tell which was which. But fancy, even now, there are still people who mix her up with her dead husband when they offer their condolences. Did you know her, dear?

Mr Smith: I only saw her once, quite by chance, at Bobby's funeral.

Mrs Smith: I've never seen her. Is she nice-looking?

Mr Smith: She has regular features, but you can't call her beautiful. She's too tall and too well-built. Her features are rather irregular, but everyone calls her beautiful. A trifle too short and too slight perhaps. She teaches singing.

[*The clock strikes five times*]

Mrs Smith: And when are they thinking of getting married, the two of them?

Mr Smith: Next spring, at the latest.

Mrs Smith: We can't possibly get out of going to their wedding·

Mr Smith: We shall have to give them a wedding present. I wonder what.

Mrs Smith: Why shouldn't we offer them one of the silver trays we were given when we were married and which have never been the slightest use to us? [*Pause*] It's sad for her to have been widowed so young.

Mr Smith: Lucky they didn't have any children.

Mrs Smith: Oh! That would have been too much! Children! What on earth would she have done with them?

Mr Smith: She's still a young woman. She may quite well marry again. Anyway, mourning suits her extremely well.

Mrs Smith: But who will take care of the children? They've a girl and a boy, you know. How do they call them?

MR SMITH: Bobby and Bobby—like their parents. Bobby
Watson's uncle, old Bobby Watson, has pots of money and
he's very fond of the boy. He could very easily take over
Bobby's education.

MRS SMITH: Yes, it's what one would expect. And in the
same way Bobby Watson's aunt, old Bobby Watson, could
very easily take over the education of Bobby Watson, the
daughter of Bobby Watson. Then, if that happened Bobby,
the mother of Bobby Watson, could marry again. Has she
anyone in view?

MR SMITH: Yes, a cousin of Bobby Watson's.

MRS SMITH: Who? Not Bobby Watson?

MR SMITH: To which Bobby Watson are you referring?

MRS SMITH: Why, to Bobby Watson, the son of old Bobby
Watson, the other uncle of the Bobby Watson who's just
died.

MR SMITH: No, it's not that one. It's another one. It's the
Bobby Watson who's the son of old Bobby Watson, the
aunt of the Bobby Watson who's just died.

MRS SMITH: Oh! You mean Bobby Watson, the commercial
traveller?

MR SMITH: They're *both* commercial travellers.

MRS SMITH: What a hard job that is! They do well out of it,
though!

MR SMITH: Yes, when there's no competition.

MRS SMITH: And when isn't there any competition?

MR SMITH: Tuesdays, Thursdays and Tuesdays.

MRS SMITH: Ah! Three days in the week? And what does
Bobby Watson do on those days?

MR SMITH: He has a rest; he sleeps.

MRS SMITH: But if there's no competition on those days, why
doesn't he work?

MR SMITH: You can't expect me to know everything. I can't
answer all your silly questions!

MRS SMITH [*hurt*]: You said that just to upset me!

MR SMITH: You know perfectly well I didn't.

MRS SMITH: You men are all alike! There you sit, all day long, with a cigarette in your mouth, making your face up with lipstick and powder fifty times a day, that is if you can take the time off from drinking!

MR SMITH: I'd like to know what you'd say if men carried on as women do! Smoking all day long, sticking powder and lipstick all over their faces and gulping down the whisky!

MRS SMITH: You can say what you like! I don't care! But if you're saying that just to get my goat, well . . . I don't like that kind of joke, you know perfectly well I don't!

[*She hurls the socks away and shows her teeth. She gets up*]

MR SMITH [*also coming to his feet and going towards his wife tenderly*]: Why are you spitting fire like that, my little roast chicken? You know I only said it for fun. [*He takes her by the waist and kisses her*] What a ridiculous couple of old love-birds we are! Come along now, we'll put the lights out and go bye-byes!

[*Enter* MARY]

MARY: I am the maid. I have just spent a very pleasant after-noon. I went to the pictures with a man and saw a film with some women. When we came out of the cinema we went and drank some brandy and some milk, and afterwards we read the newspaper.

MRS SMITH: I hope you spent a pleasant afternoon. I hope you went to the pictures with a man and drank some brandy and some milk.

MR SMITH: And the newspaper!

MARY: Your guests, Mr and Mrs Martin, are waiting at the door. They were waiting for me. They were afraid to come in on their own. They were meant to be dining with you this evening.

MRS SMITH: Ah yes. We were expecting them. And we were hungry. As they showed no sign of coming, we went and dined without them. We'd had nothing to eat all day long. You shouldn't have gone off like that, Mary.

MARY: But you gave me your permission!

MR SMITH: We didn't do it on purpose!

MARY [*bursts into laughter, then into tears. Smiling*]: I've bought myself a chamber-pot.

MRS SMITH: Dear little Mary, will you be so good as to open the door, please, and let Mr and Mrs Martin in. We'll go and get dressed quickly.

[MR *and* MRS SMITH *go off right,* MARY *opens the door left, and* MR *and* MRS MARTIN *come in*]

MARY: What do you mean by being so terribly late? It's not polite. You must arrive punctually. Understand? Still, now you're here, you might as well sit down and wait. [*She goes out.*

MR *and* MRS MARTIN *sit down opposite each other without saying a word. They exchange shy smiles.*

The following dialogue should be spoken in a drawling mono-tonous voice, rather sing-song, without light and shade]

MR MARTIN: I beg pardon, Madam, but it seems to me, if I'm not mistaken, that I have met you somewhere before.

MRS MARTIN: It seems to me too, Sir, that I have met you somewhere before.

MR MARTIN: Could it possibly be, Madam, that I've caught sight of you in Manchester?

MRS MARTIN: That is quite possible, Sir, since I come from the city of Manchester. But I have no clear recollection and I could not really say whether I have caught sight of you there or not.

MR MARTIN: Goodness gracious! How very extraordinary! I too come from the city of Manchester, Madam.

MRS MARTIN: How very extraordinary!

MR MARTIN: How very extraordinary! . . . Only, Madam, *I* left the city of Manchester five weeks ago precisely.

MRS MARTIN: How very extraordinary! What an amazing

coincidence! I too left the city of Manchester five weeks ago precisely!

MR MARTIN: I caught the train that leaves Manchester at 8.30 a.m. and arrives in London at 4.45 p.m. exactly, Madam.

MRS MARTIN: How very extraordinary! How very amazing! And what a strange coincidence! I caught the very same train, Sir!

MR MARTIN: Good gracious, how very extraordinary! Then perhaps it's possible, Madam, that I saw you in the train?

MRS MARTIN: It's not impossible, it's not out of the question, it's even plausible, and after all, why not? . . . But I have absolutely no recollection of it, Sir!

MR MARTIN: I was travelling third class, Madam. In England now there is no third class, but I always travel third class just the same.

MRS MARTIN: How very amazing! How very extraordinary and what a strange coincidence! I too, Sir, was travelling third class!

MR MARTIN: How very extraordinary! Then perhaps, dear Madam, we might have met in the third class!

MRS MARTIN: It's really quite possible and not at all out of the question. But I have no very clear recollection of it, Sir!

MR MARTIN: My seat was in carriage No. 8, the sixth compartment, Madam.

MRS MARTIN: How very extraordinary! My seat was also in carriage No. 8, the sixth compartment, Sir!

MR MARTIN: How very extraordinary and what an amazing coincidence! Perhaps, dear Madam, we could have met in the sixth compartment!

MRS MARTIN: But after all, it's not impossible! Yet I have no recollection of it, Sir.

MR MARTIN: To tell the truth, dear Madam, I have no recollection of it either, but it is possible that we caught sight of one another there, and the more I think about it, the more it all seems even *very* possible.

Mrs Martin: Oh yes, indeed, certainly, indeed, Sir!

Mr Martin: How very extraordinary! . . . I had seat No. 3 next to the window, dear Madam.

Mrs Martin: Oh good gracious, how very extraordinary and how very amazing! I had seat No. 6 next to the window right opposite you, Sir!

Mr Martin: Oh good gracious, how very extraordinary and what a strange coincidence! Then we were sitting right opposite each other, dear lady! So that's where we must have seen each other!

Mrs Martin: How very extraordinary! It is possible! But I have no recollection of it, Sir.

Mr Martin: To tell the truth, dear Madam, I have no recollection of it either. However, it's very possible that we saw each other on that occasion.

Mrs Martin: What you say is true, Sir, but I'm not at all sure about it.

Mr Martin: Was it not you, dear Madam, the lady who asked me to put her case up on the rack and who thanked me afterwards and gave me permission to smoke?

Mrs Martin: But of course, it must have been I, Sir! How very extraordinary, how very amazing and what a strange coincidence!

Mr Martin: How very extraordinary, how very amazing and what a strange coincidence! But then, but then, perhaps it was then that we met each other, dear lady.

Mrs Martin: How very extraordinary and what a strange coincidence! It's very possible, Sir! And yet I don't seem to have any recollection.

Mr Martin: Neither do I, Madam.

[*A moment's silence. The clock strikes two and a half times*]

Mr Martin: Since I arrived in London, I have been living in Broomfield Street, dear Madam.

Mrs Martin: How very extraordinary, how very amazing!

Since I came to London, I too have been living in Broom-field Street, Sir.

MR MARTIN: How very extraordinary! But then, but then, perhaps it was in Broomfield Street that we met, dear lady.

MRS MARTIN: How very extraordinary! How very amazing! After all, it's quite possible. But I have no recollection of it, Sir.

MR MARTIN: I live at Number 19, dear lady.

MRS MARTIN: How very extraordinary! I too live at Number 19, Sir!

MR MARTIN: But then, but then, but then, but then, but then, perhaps it's in that house that we met, dear lady.

MRS MARTIN: It's quite possible, Sir, but I have no clear recollection of it.

MR MARTIN: I have a flat on the fifth floor, flat Number 8, dear lady.

MRS MARTIN: How very extraordinary! Oh goodness gracious, how very amazing and what a strange coinci-dence! I too live on the fifth floor, Sir, in flat Number 8!

MR MARTIN [thoughtfully]: How very extraordinary, how very extraordinary, how very extraordinary and what a strange coincidence! You know, in my bedroom there is a bed. And on my bed is a green eiderdown. And my bedroom, with its bed and its green eiderdown, is at the end of the corridor, between the W.C. and the library, dear lady.

MRS MARTIN: What a coincidence! Oh goodness gracious, what a strange coincidence! In my bedroom too there is a bed with a green eiderdown, and it is at the end of the cor-ridor, between the W.C., Sir, and the library.

MR MARTIN: Goodness, how strange, how amazing, how extraordinary! Then, Madam, we must live in the same room and sleep in the same bed, dear Madam. Perhaps that is where we have met before!

MRS MARTIN: How very extraordinary and what a strange

coincidence! It's quite possible that is where we have met, and perhaps even last night. But I have no clear recollection of it, Sir!

MR MARTIN: Dear lady, I have a little daughter and my little daughter lives with me. She is two years old; she has fair hair, and she has one red eye and one white eye; she is very pretty and her name is Alice, dear lady.

MRS MARTIN: But what an amazing coincidence! I too have a little daughter and she is two years old and she has one red eye and one white eye; and she is very pretty and her name is Alice too, Sir!

MR MARTIN [*same drawling monotonous voice*]: How very extraordinary and what a strange coincidence! And amazing! Could it be that she is one and the same, dear Madam?

MRS MARTIN: How very extraordinary! But it's quite quite possible, Sir!

[*A rather long silence. The clock strikes twenty-nine. MR MARTIN, after considerable reflection, gets up slowly and, without haste, moves towards MRS MARTIN, who, surprised by MR MARTIN's solemn look, has risen quietly to her feet as well*]

MR MARTIN [*speaking in the same peculiar, monotonous, rather sing-song voice*]: Then, dear lady, I think there can be no mistake. We must have seen each other before and you are my very own little wife. . . . Elizabeth, I've found you again!

[*MRS MARTIN moves towards MR MARTIN without haste; they kiss without emotion. The clock strikes one very loud. So loud that it should make the audience jump. The happy pair do not notice it*]

MRS MARTIN: Donald darling, it's really you!

[*They sit down in the same armchair, still kissing, and go to sleep. The clock strikes a few times again. MARY comes in quietly, her finger to her lips, on tip-toe, and addresses the audience*]

MARY: Elizabeth and Donald are now far too happy to be able to hear me. So I can tell you a secret. Elizabeth is not Elizabeth and Donald is not Donald. And I'll prove it to you. The child Donald talked of is not Elizabeth's daughter, not the same child at all. Donald's little girl has one red eye and one white eye just like Elizabeth's little girl. But whereas it's the right eye of Donald's child that's red and the left eye that's white, it's the left eye of Elizabeth's child that's red and the right eye that's white. Consequently the whole fabric of Donald's argumentation falls to the ground, when it encounters this final obstacle, which annihilates his entire theory. In spite of the extraordinary coincidence, which would appear incontrovertible evidence to the contrary, as Donald and Elizabeth are not after all the parents of the same child, they are not, in fact, Donald and Elizabeth. Donald may well believe he is Donald; Elizabeth may well think she is Elizabeth. Donald may well believe her to be Elizabeth; Elizabeth may well think him to be Donald: they are both grievously deceived. But who is the real Donald? Which is the real Elizabeth? Who can possibly be interested in prolonging this misunderstanding? I haven't the slightest idea. Let us make no attempt to find out. Let us leave things strictly alone.

[*She takes several steps towards the door, then returns and addresses the audience again*]

My real name is Sherlock Holmes. [*She goes out.* MR *and* MRS SMITH *come in from the right. They are still wearing the same clothes*]

MRS SMITH: Good evening! How nice to see you! Please forgive us for keeping you waiting so long. We thought we ought to pay you the honours you have a right to expect, and as soon as we learnt that you were going to be kind enough to give us the pleasure of coming to see us, without announcing your intended visit, we hurried to go and put on our glad-rags.

MR SMITH: We've had nothing to eat all day. We've been expecting you for four hours. Why have you come so late?

[MR and MRS SMITH sit down opposite their visitors. Conversation is difficult and words are at first very hard to find. At the beginning a long, embarrassed silence; then later more silences and much hesitation. The clock echoes the various remarks, with more or less violence, as the case demands]

MR SMITH: Hm! [Silence]

MRS SMITH: Hm! Hm! [Silence]

MRS MARTIN: Hm! Hm! Hm! [Silence]

MR MARTIN: Hm! Hm! Hm! Hm! [Silence]

MRS MARTIN: Oh! Really! [Silence]

MR MARTIN: I think we must all have colds. [Silence]

MR SMITH: It's not cold weather, though. [Silence]

MRS SMITH: There are no draughts. [Silence]

MR MARTIN: Oh, no! Rather not! [Silence]

MR SMITH: Oh dear, oh dear, oh dear! [Silence]

MR MARTIN: Is there anything wrong? [Silence]

MRS SMITH: He can't control himself when he's bored stiff.[1]

[Silence]

MRS MARTIN: Oh really, Sir, you shouldn't at your age.

[Silence]

MR SMITH: Age doesn't count where the heart's concerned.

[Silence]

MR MARTIN: Is that true? [Silence]

MRS SMITH: That's what they say. [Silence]

[1] (Translator's note: The French is 'Il s'emmerde'. There being no English equivalent to render the two meanings, the translation must be 'strong' or 'weak' according to taste. Unless one drops one of the meanings entirely, the translation is bound to be flabby compared to the French.)

Mrs Martin: They say the contrary's true, too. [*Silence*]

Mr Smith: The truth lies between the two. [*Silence*]

Mr Martin: That's true, too. [*Silence*]

Mrs Smith [*to the* Martins]: You two are always travelling around, after all you ought to have some interesting stories to tell us.

Mr Martin [*to his wife*]: Tell them, darling, what you saw today.

Mrs Martin: Oh no, I couldn't. They'd never believe me.

Mr Smith: You don't think we'd doubt your word!

Mrs Smith: We should be very offended if you thought that.

Mr Martin [*to his wife*]: You'll upset them, darling, if you make them think . . .

Mrs Martin [*graciously*]: Well, then! Today I witnessed the most extraordinary incident. It was absolutely incredible.

Mr Martin: Tell them quickly, darling.

Mr Smith: Ah! Someone's going to make us laugh!

Mrs Smith: At last!

Mrs Martin: Well then, today, as I was going to the market to buy some vegetables, which are still going up and up in price . . .

Mrs Smith: Yes, where on earth's it going to end!

Mr Smith: You mustn't interrupt, my dear. Naughty girl!

Mrs Martin: In the street, outside a restaurant, I saw a gentleman, respectably dressed and about fifty years old, perhaps less, who was . . .

Mr Smith: Who was what?

Mrs Smith: Who was what?

Mr Smith [*gallantly to his wife*]: Mustn't interrupt, my dear, it's disgraceful of you.

Mrs Smith [*all smiles*]: You interrupted first, skunk.

Mr Martin: Ssh! [*To his wife*]: Tell them what the gentleman was doing.

Mrs Martin: Well, I know you'll say that I'm making it up: he was kneeling on the ground and leaning forward.

Mr Martin: ⎫
Mrs Smith: ⎬ Oh!
Mr Smith: ⎭

Mrs Martin: Yes! Leaning forward!

Mr Martin: ⎫
Mrs Smith: ⎬ It can't be true!
Mr Smith: ⎭

Mrs Martin: Yes! Leaning forward he was! I went right up to him to see what he was doing . . .

Mr Martin: ⎫
Mrs Smith: ⎬ What? What?
Mr Smith: ⎭

Mrs Martin: His shoe-laces had come undone and he was tying them up!

Mr Martin: ⎫
Mrs Smith: ⎬ Fantastic!
Mr Smith: ⎭

Mr Smith: If I'd heard that from anyone else, I'd never have believed it.

Mr Martin: Why not? There are even stranger things than that to be seen about the town. Only today, for example, I was in an Underground train, and there was a gentleman, sitting there as large as life and calmly reading a newspaper.

Mrs Smith: What an odd character!

Mr Smith: Perhaps it was the same gentleman!

[*The front-door bell rings*]

Listen! There's a ring at the door!

Mrs Smith: There must be someone there. I'll go and see. [*She goes to see, opens and closes the door*] Nobody! [*She sits down again*]

Mr Martin: I'll give you another example . . .

[*The bell rings again*]

Mr Smith: Listen! There's a ring at the door!

Mrs Smith: That *must* be someone. I'll go and see. [*She goes*

56

to see. She opens and closes the door again] Nobody! [*She comes back to her seat*]

MR MARTIN [*who has forgotten where he got to*]: Er . . .

MRS MARTIN: You were saying you were going to give us another example.

MR MARTIN: Oh, yes . . .

[*The bell rings again*]

MR SMITH: Listen! There's a ring at the door!

MRS SMITH: I'm not going to open it any more.

MR SMITH: Yes, but there must be someone there!

MRS SMITH: The first time there was nobody there. Nor the second time either. What makes you think there'll be someone there this time?

MR SMITH: Because there's a ring at the door.

MRS MARTIN: That's no reason.

MR SMITH: What do you mean! When you hear a ring at the bell, it's because there is someone at the door, who rings the bell so that someone else can go and answer it.

MRS MARTIN: No, not always. You saw what happened just now!

MR MARTIN: Usually there is someone there.

MR SMITH: Take myself: when I go to visit someone I ring the bell so that I can get in. I should say everybody does the same thing, and that every time there's a ring at the bell, it's because there is somebody there.

MRS SMITH: Oh yes, that's all right in theory. But in practice, things don't turn out that way at all. You saw what just happened!

MRS MARTIN: Your wife is perfectly right!

MR MARTIN: Oh! You women! Trust you to stick together!

MRS SMITH: All right then! I *will* go and look, I won't have you saying I'm pigheaded: but you'll see! There'll be nobody there! [*She goes to see. She opens and closes the door again*] What did I tell you? Nobody! [*She comes back to her seat*] Oh, these men! They're always so sure they're in the right and they're always in the wrong!

[*The bell rings again*]

Mr Smith: Listen! There's a ring at the door! There must be someone there.

Mrs Smith [*losing her temper*]: Don't go sending me to answer the door again. You've just seen it's not a bit of use. I've learnt from experience that when you hear a ring at the door, it means that there's never anybody there.

Mrs Martin: Never.

Mr Martin: I'm not sure if that's quite true.

Mr Smith: I'm quite sure it isn't. When you hear a ring at the door, it generally means that there's somebody there.

Mrs Smith: He never likes to admit he's wrong.

Mrs Martin: My husband's just as obstinate.

Mr Smith: Somebody there.

Mr Martin: It's not impossible.

Mrs Smith [*to her husband*]: There isn't.

Mr Smith: There is.

Mrs Smith: I tell you there isn't. Anyway, I'm not budging again for nothing! If you want to find out, go and look for yourself!

Mr Smith: I jolly well *shall* go! And you'll see; there'll be somebody there.

[Mrs Smith *shrugs her shoulders.*
Mrs Martin *shakes her head.*

Mr Smith *goes to the door. He throws a glance at his wife and the* Martins, *who are all taken aback*]: It's the Captain of the Fire Brigade.

[*Enter the* Fire-Chief]

Fire-Chief [*of course he is wearing a uniform and has an enormous helmet*]: Good day, all.

[*Everyone is still very surprised.* Mrs Smith *angrily turns away her head and does not return his greeting*]

Good day, Mrs Smith. You look as if something had upset you.

Mrs Smith: Oh!

Mr Smith: You see it's just that .... my wife is rather put out at being proved in the wrong.

Mr Martin: My dear Sir, there's been a slight argument between Mr and Mrs Smith.

Mrs Smith [*to* Mr Martin]: It's none of your business. [*To* Mr Smith]: Please don't let outsiders get mixed up in our family quarrels.

Mr Smith: Oh, my dear, it's really not so serious as all that. The Captain is an old friend of the family. I used to know his father, and his mother came courting me once. His father asked me for my daughter's hand in marriage, if ever I should have one. But he died too soon.

Mr Martin: That wasn't his fault, nor yours either.

Fire-Chief: Tell me, then, what the deuce was this argument about?

Mrs Smith: My husband claimed . . .

Mr Smith: Oh, no, it was you who did the claiming.

Mr Martin: Oh yes, it was she . . .

Mrs Martin: No, it was he . . .

Fire-Chief: Now, don't all get so excited. You tell me all about it, Mrs Smith.

Mrs Smith: Very well, then. I feel very embarrassed, having to talk to you so frankly, but I suppose a fireman is something of a parson, too.

Fire-Chief: Come along, now.

Mrs Smith: We were arguing because my husband said that when there's a ring at the door, there's always someone there.

Mr Martin: Sounds plausible enough, eh?

MRS SMITH: And I said that every time there's a ring at the door, it means there's nobody there.

MRS MARTIN: It may sound rather peculiar . . .

MRS SMITH: But I've been proved right, not by any theoretical arguments, but by facts.

MR SMITH: That's not true, because the fireman's here. He rang the bell, I opened the door and there he was.

MRS MARTIN: When?

MR MARTIN: But just now.

MRS SMITH: Yes, but it was only after we heard the fourth ring at the door that we found someone there. And the fourth time doesn't count.

MRS MARTIN: It's always only the first three times that count.

MR SMITH: My dear Sir, will you allow me to ask *you* some questions?

FIRE-CHIEF: Go ahead.

MR SMITH: When I opened the door and saw you there, was it actually you who rang the bell?

FIRE-CHIEF: Oh yes, it was me, all right.

MR MARTIN: You were there at the door and you rang the bell to come in?

FIRE-CHIEF: I can't deny it.

MR SMITH [*victoriously to his wife*]: You see, my dear? I was right. When there's a ring at the door, it means that there's somebody there. You can't say the Captain's nobody.

MRS SMITH: Of course not. But I repeat, I'm only talking about the first three times, since the fourth time doesn't count.

MRS MARTIN: And the first time there was a ring, was that you, too?

FIRE-CHIEF: No, that wasn't me.

MRS MARTIN: There you are! There was a ring at the bell and there was nobody there.

MR MARTIN: Perhaps it was somebody else?

MR SMITH: Had you been waiting at the door a long time?

FIRE-CHIEF: Oh, about three-quarters of an hour!

MR SMITH: But you didn't see anybody else?

FIRE-CHIEF: Nobody, I'm positive.

MRS MARTIN: Did you hear a ring the second time?

FIRE-CHIEF: Yes, but that wasn't me either. There was still nobody there.

MRS SMITH: Victory! I was right!

MR SMITH: Not so fast, my dear! [*To the* FIRE-CHIEF] And what were you doing at the door?

FIRE-CHIEF: Nothing at all. I was just standing there. I was thinking about this and that.

MR MARTIN: But the third time . . . wasn't it you who rang the third time?

FIRE-CHIEF: Yes, that was me.

MR SMITH: And when the door was opened you weren't to be seen?

FIRE-CHIEF: That was because I was hiding . . . for a joke.

MRS SMITH: It's no joke, Captain . . . This is a serious business.

MR MARTIN: In fact, we still don't know if there is anybody at the door when the bell rings or not?

MRS SMITH: Never anybody.

MR SMITH: Always somebody.

FIRE-CHIEF: I'll show you how to straighten things out. You see, really you're both right. When there's a ring at the door, sometimes it means that there's someone there and sometimes it means that there's no one there.

MR MARTIN: That seems logical enough to me.

MRS MARTIN: To me, too.

FIRE-CHIEF: Everything's very simple, really. Come on now, kiss and make up.

MRS SMITH: But we kissed and made up only a few moments ago.

MR MARTIN: Oh, they can kiss and make up tomorrow. They've all the time in the world.

MRS SMITH: Please make yourself comfortable, now you've

just helped us to put all that right. Do take off your helmet and sit down a moment.

FIRE-CHIEF: I'm sorry, but I can't stay very long. I'll be glad to take off my helmet, but I really haven't the time to sit down. [*He sits down without taking off his helmet*] I must admit I came to see you on quite a different matter. I really came on duty.

MRS SMITH: Oh, please tell us, then, what we can do to help you.

FIRE-CHIEF: I'm terribly sorry, but I must ask you first if you would be so kind as to be willing to excuse my being a trifle indiscreet. [*Very embarrassed*]: Er . . . er . . . [*He points at the* MARTINS] May I perhaps . . . in front of them . . .

MRS MARTIN: Oh, please don't pay any attention to us.

MR MARTIN: We're very old friends and they tell us *everything*.

MR SMITH: Please go on.

FIRE-CHIEF: Well then, here goes. Have you by any chance a fire in the house?

MRS SMITH: Why do you ask that?

FIRE-CHIEF: It's because . . . I really do beg your pardon, but I have orders to extinguish all the fires in the town.

MRS MARTIN: All of them?

MRS SMITH [*confused*]: I really couldn't say . . . I don't think so. Would you like me to go and see?

MR SMITH [*sniffing*]: Theredoesn't seem to be one, I can't smell anything burning.

FIRE-CHIEF [*very disappointed*]: Nothing at all? You wouldn't even have a tiny little chimney fire somewhere, something smouldering in the attic perhaps or in the cellar? Not even a wee little beginning of a fire?

MRS SMITH: Oh, please understand. I so hate to disappoint you, but honestly I'm afraid you'll find nothing here for the moment. I promise to let you know as soon as there is something.

FIRE-CHIEF: Oh, please do that, you'd really be doing me a favour.

MRS SMITH: It's a promise.

FIRE-CHIEF [to the MARTINS]: And there's nothing burning at your place, either?

MRS MARTIN: No, unfortunately.

MR MARTIN [to the FIRE-CHIEF]: Business must be going rather badly at the moment!

FIRE-CHIEF: Very badly. There's hardly anything at all; a few piffling little jobs, a chimney or a barn on fire. Nothing serious at all. It just doesn't bring enough in. And as production is almost at a standstill the bonus on a high output is practically negligible.

MR SMITH: Yes, business is bad this year. It's the same everywhere. Commerce and agriculture are not doing well either, just like the fire business.

MR MARTIN: No wheat and no fires.

FIRE-CHIEF: Not even any floods.

MRS SMITH: But there *is* some sugar.

MR SMITH: That's because they've imported some from abroad.

MRS MARTIN: But when it comes to fires it's more difficult. They're too highly taxed.

FIRE-CHIEF: Anyhow, there are, luckily, though this is pretty rare too, one or two cases of asphyxiation by gas. Last week, for instance, there was a young girl who asphyxiated herself. She had left the gas on.

MRS MARTIN: She'd forgotten it?

FIRE-CHIEF: No, she thought it was her comb.

MR SMITH: Mistakes like that are always very dangerous.

MRS SMITH: Have you been round to have a look at the matchmaker's?

FIRE-CHIEF: Nothing doing. He's insured against fires.

MR MARTIN: Why don't you go and see my old friend the Vicar of Wakefield?

FIRE-CHIEF: I haven't the right to put out a parson's fire. It would annoy the bishop. They usually put out their own fires, or else they get their vestals to do it for them.

MR SMITH: Why not try Durand's place?

FIRE-CHIEF: I can't do that either. He's not English. He's only naturalized. People who are naturalized have the right to own their houses but not to put them out if they start burning.

MRS SMITH: And yet last year when it caught fire, it was put out just the same!

FIRE-CHIEF: He did that all by himself. On the quiet. But I'm not the one to go and denounce him.

MR SMITH: Neither am I.

MRS SMITH: As you're in no hurry, why don't you stay a little longer? We'd be very pleased.

FIRE-CHIEF: Would you like me to tell you some stories?

MRS SMITH: Oh yes! Oh yes! What a charming man you are!

[*She kisses him*]

MR SMITH:
MR MARTIN: } Yes, yes, some stories, bravo, bravo. [*They clap their hands*]
MRS MARTIN:

MR SMITH: And what's specially interesting about it is that a fireman's stories are always real live ones.

FIRE-CHIEF: Yes, I usually tell about things that I've experienced myself. Nature, nothing but nature, you know. None of those books.

MR MARTIN: True, very true. Truth lies not in books but in life.

MRS SMITH: Do begin!

MR MARTIN: Do begin!

MRS MARTIN: Ssh! He's beginning.

FIRE-CHIEF [*after several coughs*]: I'm very sorry, but please don't all look at me like that. You're making me nervous. You know how shy I am.

MRS SMITH: What a charming man! [*She kisses him*]

FIRE-CHIEF: Still, I'll try to begin. But promise me you won't listen.

MRS MARTIN: But if we don't listen, we won't hear you.

FIRE-CHIEF: I'd never thought of that.

MR SMITH: ⎱
MRS SMITH: ⎰ Oh, what a dear boy!
MR MARTIN: ⎱

MRS MARTIN: Courage!

FIRE-CHIEF: Very well, then. [*He coughs again and then starts in a voice trembling with emotion*] The Dog and the Ox. An experimental fable. Once upon a time, another ox asked another dog a question. Why haven't you swallowed your trunk? I beg your pardon, replied the dog, I always thought I was an elephant.

MRS MARTIN: Wh . . . What is the moral?

FIRE-CHIEF: It's for you to discover it.

MR SMITH: He's perfectly right.

MRS SMITH: Tell us a different one.

FIRE-CHIEF: A young calf had eaten too much ground glass. As a result he had to be confined. He gave birth to a cow. But as the calf was a boy, the cow couldn't call him 'mother'. She couldn't say 'father' to him either as he wasn't big enough. So the calf was obliged to get married to a certain young person, and the registry office made all the arrangements dictated by the current conventions.

MR SMITH: Cornish conventions.

MR MARTIN: Like pasties.

FIRE-CHIEF: You know my story then?

MRS SMITH: It was in all the papers.

MRS MARTIN: It happened not far from where we live.

FIRE-CHIEF: Well, I'll tell you another. The Cock: Once upon a time a cock wanted to ape a dog. But he didn't have any luck, because everyone knew at once it was a cock.

Mrs Smith: Yes, but on the other hand the dog that wanted to ape a cock was taken for an ape.

Mr Smith: Now I'd like to tell you one, too.

The Snake and the Fox[1]: One day a snake went up to a fox and said to him: I know you! Give me some money. A fox never gives away his money, the cunning animal replied, and, running away, leapt down into a deep valley, full of strawberry bushes and hen's honey. But the snake was already there waiting for him. He planted himself in front of the fox and gave a Mephistophelian laugh. The fox quickly extracted a knife from his bosom, uttered a peal of derisive laughter, and then, turning his back, took to his heels. But the snake was too quick for him. With a well-aimed blow of his fist he struck the fox full in the forehead and smashed it to smithereens, crying as he did so: No! No! Ninety-nine times, No! I'm not your bit of fluff!

Mrs Martin: That's interesting!

Mrs Smith: Not bad at all!

Mrs Martin: Allow me to congratulate you!

Fire-Chief [*jealously*]: Not up to much! And then I'd heard it before!

Mrs Smith: Yes, it was a terrible thing!

Mr Martin: But it wasn't a true story?

Mrs Smith: Oh yes, unfortunately it was.

Mr Martin [*after a moment of anguished silence, to* Mrs Smith]: It's your turn, Mrs Smith.

Mrs Smith: I only know one story. But I'll tell it to you. It's called 'The Bouquet'.

Mr Smith: Yes, my wife has always been romantically minded.

Mr Martin: She's a true-blue Englishwoman.

Mrs Smith: Well . . .

[1] (Author's Note: In the production of N. Bataille this anecdote was simply mimed by Mr Smith.)

MR SMITH: Yes, my wife has always been romantically minded.

MR MARTIN: She's a true-blue Englishwoman.

MRS SMITH: Well . . .

MR SMITH: Yes, my wife has always been romantically minded.

MR MARTIN: She's a true-blue Englishwoman.

MRS MARTIN: Well . . .

MRS SMITH: The Bouquet: Once upon a time a gentleman took his fiancée some flowers and she thanked him for them. But before she had time to thank him, he took back the flowers he'd just given her, to give her a good lesson, and as he took them away, he walked away in two directions at once.

MR MARTIN: Charming.

MRS MARTIN: Absolutely everybody, Mr Smith, is jealous of you for having such a wife.

MR SMITH: It's true, my wife is intelligence itself; she is even more intelligent than I am. At least, they say she's a lot more feminine.

MRS SMITH [to the FIRE-CHIEF]: Please tell us another one.

FIRE-CHIEF: No. It's too late now.

MRS SMITH: Tell us one all the same.

FIRE-CHIEF: And then I'm much too tired.

MR SMITH: Do it to please us.

MR MARTIN: Oh please do.

FIRE-CHIEF: No.

MRS MARTIN: You have a heart like an icicle. We're on hot bricks.

MRS SMITH: I implore you.

FIRE-CHIEF: All right, then.

MR SMITH: There we are. He agrees. He's going to bore us again.

MRS MARTIN: Damn.

MRS SMITH: Serves me right for being too polite.

FIRE-CHIEF: The Cold: My brother-in-law had, on his father's side, a first cousin whose maternal uncle had a father-in-law whose paternal grandfather had in second marriage married a young native girl whose brother had met, during one of his voyages, a girl with whom he fell in love and by whom he had a son who married a gallant governess who was no other than the niece of an obscure leading seaman in the British Navy, whose adoptive father had an aunt who spoke fluent Spanish, and who was probably one of the grand-daughters of an engineer who died young, who was the grandson of a vine-grower, whose wine was excessively poor, but who had married an extremely handsome young woman, twice divorced, whose first husband was the son of a sincere patriot who, having brought up one of his daughters in the idea of making her fortune, managed to marry her off to a commissionaire who once knew Roths-child, and whose brother, after changing his job several times, got married and had a son who took for his wife a girl whose great-grandfather was an albino, who used to wear spectacles given to him by one of his cousins, foster-brother to a Portuguese, natural son of a milkman, not badly off, whose brother-in-law had married the daughter of a retired country doctor, who was himself brother-in-law to the son of a lawyer who was a natural son of another country doctor, married three times, whose third wife . . .

MR MARTIN: I used to know his third wife, if I'm not mistaken. She used to eat chicken in her bee-hive.

FIRE-CHIEF: It wasn't the same one.

MRS SMITH: Be quiet!

FIRE-CHIEF: As I was saying: whose third wife was the daughter of the best midwife in the district, who, widowed early in her marriage . . .

MR SMITH: Like my wife.

FIRE-CHIEF: . . . had got married again, to a publican, a man full of spirit, who got by child the daughter of a stationmaster, and this child learnt how to play the game of life . . .

MR MARTIN: Bridge for instance . . .

MRS SMITH: Railway Bridge.

FIRE-CHIEF: . . . and had married a costermongeress, whose father had a brother, the mayor of a small town, who took as his wife a blonde schoolmistress, whose cousin, a compleat angler . . .

MR MARTIN: A complete wangler?

FIRE-CHIEF: . . . took for a wife another blonde schoolmistress, also called Mary, whose brother was married to another Mary, who was also a blonde schoolmistress . . .

MR SMITH: Since she's a blonde, she must be a Mary.

FIRE-CHIEF: . . . whose father was brought up in Canada by an old lady who was the niece of a vicar whose grandmother used, sometimes, in winter, just like everyone else, to catch a cold.

MRS SMITH: What a strange story! Almost incredible!

MR MARTIN: In any case, when one's got a cold, one ought to take a mould.

MR SMITH: It's a useless but absolutely vital precaution.

MRS MARTIN: Please forgive me, but I didn't quite get the point of your story. Right at the end, you lose the thread, in the piece about the vicar's niece.

MR SMITH: I never cease to lose the thread of anything the vicar's said.

MRS SMITH: Oh yes! Please begin again from the beginning! Everyone wants you to.

FIRE-CHIEF: I really don't know if I can. I came on duty. It depends what the time is.

MRS SMITH: We can never tell the time here at home.

FIRE-CHIEF: But the clock?

MR SMITH: It doesn't work properly. It's of a contrary turn of mind. It always strikes the contrary to the right time.

[*Enter* MARY]

MARY: Sir . . . Madam . . .

MRS SMITH: What is it?

MR SMITH: Who told you to come in here?

MARY: I beg to be excused . . . Sir . . . Madam . . . and the other ladies and gentlemen too . . . I should like to . . . like to . . . take my turn too . . . and tell you a story.

FIRE-CHIEF: How dare she! [*Looking at her*] Oh!

MRS SMITH: What do you mean by such a thing?

MR SMITH: This isn't your proper place, in here . . .

FIRE-CHIEF: Oh! But it's not possible, it's you!

MR SMITH: You too?

MARY: Impossible! Here in this house!

MRS SMITH: What on earth does all this mean?

MR SMITH: Are you two friends?

FIRE-CHIEF: And how! I am, in a funny sort of way, her spiritual son.

MARY: I'm so happy to see you again . . . at last! at last!

MR SMITH: ⎫
⎬ Oh!
MRS SMITH: ⎭

MR SMITH: This is too much, here, in our very own home, in the suburbs of London . . .

MRS SMITH: It's not respectable!

FIRE-CHIEF: She was the first flame to put me out.

MARY: I'm just his favourite little water-spout.

MR MARTIN: But if this is really the case . . . my dear friends . . . these sentiments are explicable, human, perfectly honourable.

MRS MARTIN: Everything human is honourable.

MRS SMITH: I still don't like to see her there, as though she were one of us.

MR SMITH: She hasn't the necessary education.

FIRE-CHIEF: Oh, how bigoted you are!

MRS MARTIN: Well, it seems to me that on the whole,

although of course it's no concern of ours, a maid is always a maid . . .

MR MARTIN: Even if, at times of course, she makes a passable detective.

FIRE-CHIEF: Let me get at them!

MARY: Don't upset yourself! They're not as bad as all that.

MR SMITH: Hm! Hm! You're really somewhat touching, both of you, but still a little . . . er . . . a little . . . er . . .

MR MARTIN: You've hit it. That's the very word.

MR SMITH: A little too . . . a little *too*.

MR MARTIN: There is a certain British sense of fundamental decency, which . . . er . . . I beg you to excuse me again for trying to . . . er . . . put my opinion bluntly . . . is not understood very well by foreigners, thanks to which . . . er . . . if I may so express myself . . . I mean . . . er . . . of course I'm not saying this because of you . . . er . . .

MARY: I wanted to tell you something.

MR SMITH: There's no telling here!

MARY: Oh but yes!

MRS SMITH: My dear Mary, please be very good and run along to the kitchen and go and read your poetry there out loud in front of the mirror.

MR MARTIN: Goodness me! Although I'm not a maid, I too read poetry while I'm looking at myself in the mirror.

MRS MARTIN: And yet when you looked in the mirror this morning, you didn't see yourself.

MR MARTIN: That's because I wasn't yet there.

MARY: Perhaps I might just be allowed, all the same, to recite you one little poem.

MRS SMITH: My dear Mary, you really are incurably obstinate.

MARY: That's settled then. I'm going to recite you a little poem. It's called 'The Fire', in honour of the Captain. [*As she recites the poem*, MR *and* MRS SMITH *push her slowly from the room*]

71

'The Fire'
The polyanders were glow-worming in the wood.
A stone caught fire
The palace caught fire
The forest caught fire
Men on fire
Women on fire
Eyes on fire
The blood caught fire
The sand caught fire
The birds caught fire
The fish caught fire
The moon caught fire
The ashes caught fire
The smoke caught fire
The fire caught fire
Caught fire, caught fire, caught fire . . . caught fire . . .

MRS MARTIN: That gave me shivers down my spine.

MR MARTIN: Yet there was a certain warmth in those lines.
[*After pushing the* MAID *out of the room, the* SMITHS *come back, looking as though they had committed a crime*]

FIRE-CHIEF: I thought that was wonderful. It's so true. It's so exactly the way I think myself, just my own idea of life, my ideal way of life!

MRS SMITH: All the same!

MR SMITH: You exaggerate!

FIRE-CHIEF: Well, I must be going. In three-quarters of an hour and sixteen minutes exactly, I have a fire to attend to, at the other side of London. I must hurry. Even though it's nothing to walk home about.

MRS SMITH: What is it going to be? A little chimney fire?

FIRE-CHIEF: Not even that. A flash in a pan and a slight touch of heartburn.

MR SMITH: We are very sorry to see you go, you know.

MRS SMITH: You've been so very entertaining.

MRS MARTIN: Thanks to you we've passed a really Shavian
    quarter of an hour.
FIRE-CHIEF: By the way, what about the Bald Prima Donna?

   [*General silence, horror*]

MRS SMITH: She always wears her hair the same way!
FIRE-CHIEF: Good-bye, all.
MR MARTIN: Good luck, and Happy Firehunting!
FIRE-CHIEF: Let's hope so. For everyone's sake.

   [*The* FIRE-CHIEF *goes out. They all accompany him to the
   door, then come back and continue their conversation standing
   up*]

MRS MARTIN: I can buy a pocket-knife for my brother, but
    you could not buy Ireland for your grandfather.
MR SMITH: One walks on one's feet, but one keeps warm
    with the aid of coal and electricity.
MR MARTIN: Sell a pig today, eat an egg tomorrow.
MRS SMITH: In life you've got to look out of the window.
MRS MARTIN: You may sit down on the chair, when the chair
    hasn't any.
MR SMITH: One can always be in two places at once.
MR MARTIN: The floor is below us and the ceiling is above us.
MRS SMITH: When I say Yes, it's only a manner of speaking.
MRS MARTIN: We all have our cross to bear.
MR SMITH: Describe a circle, stroke its back and it turns
    vicious.
MRS SMITH: A schoolmaster teaches his children how to read
    but a cat feeds her little ones when they are small.
MRS MARTIN: And yet the cow gives us her beefsteaks.
MR SMITH: When I go to the country, I enjoy the peace and
    quiet.
MRS MARTIN: You're not old enough to do that yet.
MRS SMITH: George Washington was right. You're not as
    truthful as he was.

MRS MARTIN: What are the names of the seven days of the week?

MR SMITH: Lundi, mardi, mercredi, jeudi, vendredi, samedi, dimanche.

MR MARTIN: Edouard a la plume de ma tante, sa sœur Odette va à l'école, et moi je suis anglais.

MRS SMITH: What a funny family!

MRS MARTIN: I'd rather see a bird in a field than a marrow in a wheelbarrow.

MR SMITH: A haddock in a paddock is better than a crab in a lab.

MR MARTIN: An Englishman's home is his castle.

MRS SMITH: I don't know enough Spanish to make myself understood.

MRS MARTIN: I would give you the slippers of my mother-in-law if you gave me the coffin of your husband.

MR SMITH: I am looking for a monogynist priest to marry our maidservant.

MR MARTIN: The pine is a tree, whereas the pine is also a tree, and an oak breeds an oak every morning at dawn.

MRS SMITH: My uncle lives in the country, but that's none of the midwife's business.

MR MARTIN: Paper is for writing and the cat's for the rat. Cheese is for rationing.

MRS SMITH: A motor car travels very fast, but I'd rather have a cook to cook the dinner.

MR SMITH: Don't be a silly goose, kiss the conspirator instead.

MR MARTIN: Honi soit qui mal y pense.

MRS SMITH: I'm waiting for Mahomet to come to my mountain.

MR MARTIN: Social progress is much better coated with sugar.

MR SMITH: Down with polishing!

[*Immediately after this last reply of* MR SMITH'S, *the others are silenced for a moment, stupefied. There is a certain nervous*

strain in the atmosphere. The clock chimes, too, more tensely.
The dialogue that follows should start at first on an icy, hostile
tone, the hostility and the tension gradually increasing.
At the end of the scene the four characters should be standing up,
face to face, close together, shouting at each other, raising their
fists, ready to hurl themselves at each other's throats]

MR MARTIN: You can't polish your spectacles with black boot-polish.

MRS SMITH: Yes, but when you've got money, you can buy everything you want.

MR MARTIN: I'd rather slaughter a rabbit than whistle in the garden.

MR SMITH: Pistletoe, pistletoe, pistletoe, pistletoe, pistletoe, pistletoe, pistletoe, pistletoe, pistletoe, pistletoe, pistletoe.

MRS SMITH: What a pissing, what a pissing, what a pissing, what a pissing, what a pissing, what a pissing, what a pissing, what a pissing.

MR MARTIN: A shower of pities, a shower of pities, a shower of pities, a shower of pities, a shower of pities, a shower of pities, a shower of pities, a shower of pities.

MR SMITH: The dogs have got fleas, the dogs have got fleas.

MRS MARTIN: Cock fowl duck, cock fowl duck, cock fowl duck.

MRS SMITH: Cock, you're fowling us.

MR MARTIN: I'd rather lay an egg than steal an ox.

MR SMITH: Mucky duck!

MRS MARTIN [*opening her mouth wide*]: Ah! Oh! Ah! Oh! Stop grinding my teeth!

MR SMITH: Your eyes are putrefying.

MR MARTIN: Let's go and slap Ulysses.

MR SMITH: I'm off to my little hut in Cockaigne.

MRS MARTIN: The cockatoos of Cockaigne have cockeyed cockscombs! The cockatoos of Cockaigne have cockeyed cockscombs! The cockatoos of Cockaigne have cockeyed cockscombs!

Mrs Smith: The mice have got lice, the lice haven't got mice.
Mrs Martin: Leave my slipper alone!
Mr Martin: Don't slip her slipper!
Mr Smith: Slip of the lip, don't lip her slip.
Mrs Martin: The lip's slipping.
Mrs Smith: Clip your lip.
Mr Martin: Flip the slipper, lips the flipper.
Mr Smith: Flip the clipper.
Mrs Martin: Flippertigibbet!
Mrs Smith: Flippertyflapper!
Mr Martin: Your flapper's slipped.
Mr Smith: I'll slap your flipper!
Mrs Martin: Gibbertiflippet, flip my slapper.
Mr Martin: Don't flip her! She's fallen to pieces![1]
Mrs Martin: Alfred!
Mr Smith: Tennyson!
Mrs Martin:
Mr Smith: } Arthur!
Mrs Smith:
Mr Martin: } Sullivan!
Mrs Martin:
Mr Smith: } Sullivan Alfred.
Mrs Smith:
Mr Martin: } Tennyson Arthur.
Mrs Martin: You cacklegobblers! You gobblecacklers!
Mr Martin: Cat's lick and pot's luck!
Mrs Smith: Krishnawallop, Krishnawallop, Krishnawallop!
Mr Smith: The Pope's eloped! The Pope's no soap! Soap is dope!

[1] (Author's Note: In the production of Nicholas Bataille, after 'flip my slapper', Mrs Smith slaps Mrs Martin in the face. She utters a cry and falls fainting into the arms of Mr Martin. It is at this point that Mr Martin says: 'Don't flip her! She's fallen to pieces!' Mrs Martin, before fainting quite away, says: 'Alfred!' and Mr Martin: 'Tennyson!' Then Mrs Martin and Mr Martin freeze into what might be called 'the fainting position', while the Smiths continue the dialogue alone, running frantically around the stage, until the final black-out.)

MRS MARTIN: Bazaar, Baseball, Bassoon!

MR MARTIN: Business! Bosnia! Buster!

MR SMITH: Aeiou, aeiou, aeiou!

MRS MARTIN: Bcdfg, lmnpq, rstvwxz!

MR MARTIN: Do re mi fa sol la si do!

MRS MARTIN: Said the barley to the cabbage, said the cabbage to the oats!

MRS SMITH [*imitating a train*]: Puff Puff Puff Puff Puff Puff Puff Puff Puff Puff Puff Puff Puff!

MR SMITH: It's!

MRS MARTIN: Not!

MR MARTIN: That!

MRS SMITH: Way!

MR SMITH: It's!

MRS MARTIN: This!

MR MARTIN: Way!

[*All together, furiously, at the top of their bent they scream into each other's ears, until darkness falls and you can just hear, getting faster and faster*]:

ALL: It's not that way, it's this way, not that way, it's this way, not thatter way, thisser way, thatter way, thisser way, thatter way, thisser way, thatter way, thisser way, thatter way, thisser way.

[*Darkness, then peace and light*]
[MR *and* MRS MARTIN (*or* MR *and* MRS SMITH).
Repeat of start of first scene]

MRS MARTIN: Goodness! Nine o'clock! This evening for supper we had soup, fish, cold ham and mashed potatoes and a good English salad and we had English beer to drink. The children drank English water. We had a very good meal this evening. And that's because we are English, because we live in a suburb of London and because our name is Smith.

77

[MR MARTIN *goes on reading his newspaper and clicks his tongue*]

Mashed potatoes are very nice with cold ham. The mayonnaise was quite fresh. The mayonnaise from the grocer round the corner is much better quality than the mayonnaise from the grocer opposite, it's even better than the mayonnaise from the grocer at the bottom of the hill. Of course I don't mean to say that his mayonnaise is bad . . .

CURTAIN

A Resounding Tinkle

by

N. F. SIMPSON

First performed at the Royal Court Theatre,
London, on 1 December 1957. Producer, William Gaskill

Cast

BRO PARADOCK
MIDDIE PARADOCK
UNCLE TED

AUTHOR'S NOTE—From time to time parts of the play may seem to become detached from the main body. No attempt, well-intentioned or not, should be made from the auditorium to nudge these back into position while the play is in motion. They will eventually drop off and are quite harmless.

A Resounding Tinkle

SCENE: *The living-room of the Paradocks' suburban home.*
Evening. Time: the present.
A door leads to a small entrance hall, where coats and hats
are hanging. A window looks out on to the garden.
When the curtain rises, it is not yet dark, and the window
curtains are undrawn. A fire is burning in the grate. BRO *and*
MIDDIE PARADOCK *have just come in. A shopping basket full*
of books is on the coffee-table. Both BRO *and* MIDDIE *are staring*
out of the window into the garden.

MIDDIE: It'll have to stay out.

BRO [*turning away from the window*]: What are the measurements?

MIDDIE [*continuing to stare through the window*]: You don't
need measurements. A thing that size in a semi!

BRO: I thought we were living in a bungalow. [*He picks up*
two small adjustable spanners from the sideboard]

MIDDIE: People think you're trying to go one better than
everybody else.

BRO: What are these doing here? When did we order adjustable spanners?

MIDDIE: They were samples.

BRO: What do they think we want with two?

MIDDIE: One of them is probably for loosening things.

BRO: You can do that with any spanner.

MIDDIE [*with a handful of small identical books*]: I've brought in some more of these in case Uncle Ted comes. I expect he'll ask for critical essays with his coffee.

BRO [*after a pause*]: There's no difference between them. You can use either of them for tightening and you can use either of them for loosening.

MIDDIE: One is probably bigger than the other or something.

[MIDDIE *exits, leaving the door open*]

BRO: They're *adjustable*, Middie. [*He puts the spanners on the sideboard, goes to the armchair, picks up a newspaper, sits and reads*]

MIDDIE [*off*]: Or smaller or something.

BRO: The plain fact is that we don't need adjustable spanners and are never likely to. [*He pauses*] It would be interesting to know what would have happened if *I'd* answered the door and let them foist adjustable spanners on to us.

MIDDIE [*off*]: We don't have to use them if we don't like them.

BRO [*after a pause*]: We shall have them unloading a complete tool-kit on us before we know where we are.

MIDDIE [*off*]: They won't be round again.

BRO: I hope you're right—that's all I can say.

MIDDIE [*off*]: I wish it were.

[MIDDIE *enters, and as though attracted compulsively towards it, crosses to the window*]

I wish that were all you could say. Except that then we'd have you saying it all day long, I suppose, like a mentally deficient parakeet. [*She looks steadily through the window*]

BRO: What a typical woman's remark. A parakeet saying the same thing over and over again wouldn't necessarily be mentally deficient. If that's all it's been taught how can it say anything different?

MIDDIE: Look at it.

Bro: It may be educationally subnormal—but that's another matter.

Middie: Look at its great ears flapping about.

Bro [*after a pause*]: It's only once a year, for goodness sake.

Middie: Surely they know by now what size we always have.

Bro: Perhaps they've sent us the wrong one.

Middie: It's big enough for a hotel. [*She picks up a magazine from the coffee-table and sits on the sofa*] If you had a hotel or a private school or something you wouldn't need a thing that size.

Bro: I suppose not.

Middie: And supposing it goes berserk in the night? I'm not getting up to it.

Bro: Why should it go berserk any more than a smaller one?

Middie: We shall have old Mrs Stencil round again if it does —threatening us with the R.S.P.C.A.

Bro: You should have been in when they came with it, then you could have queried the measurements.

Middie: I can't think what we're going to call it. We can't call it Mr Trench again.

Bro: The only time we've not called it Mr Trench was three years ago when we had to make do with a giraffe.

Middie: And look at the fuss we had before they'd take it in part exchange.

Bro: Of course they made a fuss. There was something wrong with it.

[Middie *puts the magazine on the coffee-table, then picks up her rug-making materials and works on the rug. She does this intermittently throughout the evening*]

Middie: Imagine calling a clumsy great thing that size Mr Trench.

Bro: Why not?

MIDDIE: We can't go on year after year calling it Mr Trench

BRO: You talk as if it were the same animal every time.

MIDDIE: You can hear the neighbours, can't you? They'll think we never launch out.

BRO: I know what you want to call it.

MIDDIE: It looks all the time as if we're hard up for a name to give the animal.

BRO: You want to call it Oedipus Rex, don't you?

MIDDIE: It's better than Mr Trench year after year. At least it sounds as if we knew what was going on in the world.

BRO [*contemptuously*]: Oedipus Rex! [*He wags a finger archly through the window*] Ah, ah! Only the *edible* blooms, remember, Oedipus.

MIDDIE: If you say it in that tone of voice—of course it sounds ridiculous.

BRO: Oedipus! Not all your weight on that glass, eh?

MIDDIE: Anything would sound ridiculous if you said it like that.

BRO: It isn't Mr Trench we want a change from.

MIDDIE: The only thing to do is ring up the Zoo. Tell them to come and collect it.

BRO: And be without an elephant at all?

MIDDIE: Tell them to come and collect it and the sooner the better. I'd rather not have one.

BRO: That's only your point of view.

MIDDIE: We did without one the year we had a giraffe instead.

BRO: I know we did without one the year we had a giraffe instead. And look at the trouble we had getting it changed. I don't want that all over again.

MIDDIE: It's the R.S.P.C.A. I'm worried about.

BRO: They haven't been round yet. In any case you wouldn't get the Zoo at this time. They'll be closed.

MIDDIE: I don't know why they couldn't send us what we asked for in the first place.

BRO: Is it any use trying to get hold of Eddie on the phone?

MIDDIE: Yes. Ring Eddie up. Or Nora. Nora'd be sure to know what to do. They used to keep pigeons and things. They had a room full of nothing else but different kinds of birds when they were all living at number eighty-nine, and white mice and things.

BRO: It'll have to stay outside tonight.

MIDDIE: I'm not having it in the kitchen, if that's what you're leading up to.

BRO: If it starts straying all over the place during the night we shall have the R.S.P.C.A. making a lot of difficulties.

MIDDIE: Not if we get it changed first thing. Get on to Nora.

BRO: If we're getting it changed first thing in the morning, where's the sense in thinking up a name like Oedipus Rex for it now?

MIDDIE: Because I'm not calling it Mr Trench six years running. You can if you like. I'm not.

BRO: I didn't want to call it Mr Trench the year it was a giraffe. That was your idea. It was your idea it would make a pleasant change to give the name to a giraffe instead of an elephant. Now you complain about calling it Mr Trench six years running.

MIDDIE: I think we'd be better off without it.

BRO: How would we?

MIDDIE: I do really. I think we'd be better off without. We've done nothing except bicker ever since they came with it.

BRO: We weren't in when they came with it.

MIDDIE: That's the whole point.

[*Both relapse into silence.* BRO *reads his paper. After a few moments he looks up*]

BRO: If we're going to change the name at all, I can't see what you've got against 'Hodge' for that matter.

MIDDIE: 'Hodge' is all right for a monkey.

BRO: We'll go through some names and see what we can agree on. 'Hodge.'

MIDDIE: 'Hodge' for a monkey. 'Gush' for an elephant.

BRO: 'Admiral Benbow.'

MIDDIE: 'Hiram B. Larkspur.'

BRO: 'Playboy.'

MIDDIE: 'Killed-with-kindness Corcoran.'

BRO: 'New-wine-into-old-bottles Backhouse.'

MIDDIE: ' 'Tis-pity-she's-a-whore Hignett.'

BRO: 'Lucifer.'

MIDDIE: 'Stonehenge.'

BRO: 'Haunch.'

[*There is a pause*]

MIDDIE ⎫
BRO ⎭ [*almost simultaneously*]: 'Splinter.'

BRO: Thank goodness we can agree on something. Now I can ring Eddie. [*He puts his paper on the floor, rises, crosses to the telephone, lifts the receiver and dials a number*]

MIDDIE: Why ring Eddie when you've got Nora who's had some experience with animals? She could probably suggest something.

BRO: So you keep saying.

MIDDIE: Well?

BRO [*into the telephone*]: Is that Mrs Mortice? . . . Oh . . . Yes, will you? Tell her Bro Paradock would like a word with her. [*He waits*]

MIDDIE: You've decided to ring Nora, then?

BRO [*ignoring MIDDIE; into the telephone*]: Hallo . . . Nora? . . . Yes, thank you, Nora. And how are you? . . . Oh? . . . And what's that, Nora? . . . A what? . . . No! I can't believe it. Hold on a moment, Nora. Wait till I fetch Middie to the phone.

MIDDIE: Don't tell me they've got ours.

BRO [*to* MIDDIE]: It's her snake. It's too short.

MIDDIE: Too short for what? [*She rises, moves to* BRO *and takes the receiver from him*]

BRO: She says they're worried about the R.S.P.C.A.

MIDDIE [*into the telephone*]: Nora? . . . Yes, Bro was telling me. Isn't it maddening? . . . Yes . . . Yes . . . Yes, and do you know they've done exactly the same with us . . . No —about ten times too big. You'd think they'd know by now, wouldn't you? A thing that size in a semi of all things.

BRO: This is a bungalow, for the fiftieth time.

MIDDIE [*to* BRO]: Oh, for God's sake! [*Into the telephone*] No, Nora, I was talking to Bro. He won't have it we're living in a semi. If I've got the deeds out once to show him, I've got them out a hundred times . . .

BRO: I wouldn't have bought the place without looking pretty closely . . .

MIDDIE [*into the telephone*]: Just a moment, Nora. He's got to have his say out.

BRO: I wouldn't have bought it without looking pretty closely at the deeds to see if there was any mention of its being semi-detached. It's one of the things I always look for.

MIDDIE [*into the telephone*]: I'm sorry, Nora. I've started Bro off on his hobby-horse again . . .

BRO: You just read things into them once you've made up your mind.

MIDDIE [*into the telephone*]: He's got a thing about this being a bungalow, Nora. He hasn't set foot upstairs since we moved in . . . Exactly, Nora . . . It's just the same with us, of course. We're stuck with the thing like you . . . We shan't get the Zoo at this time . . . We shall just have to keep it till the morning . . . Not indoors, no. We've got it out at the back . . . Yes, I should think so, Nora . . . You're perfectly justified . . .

[BRO *tries to attract* MIDDIE'S *attention*]

BRO: Why not ask her if she'd like to have Mr Trench and we'll take the snake off her?

MIDDIE [*to* BRO]: What? [*Into the telephone*] No, it's something Bro just said, Nora. I think he's thought of something. I'll get him to tell you. [*She puts her hand over the mouthpiece. To* BRO] You talk to her; she's on about this snake of hers.

[BRO *takes the receiver from* MIDDIE]

BRO [*into the telephone*]: What do you say to that, Nora? . . . How about it? . . . Oh, I thought Middie told you. It was just an idea I had—I thought perhaps we could help each other out if I came round with our Mr Trench and took the snake off you . . . Are you? . . . Yes—Middie wants to change the name of ours this year . . . 'Oedipus Rex' . . . Of course it is, Nora—and for an elephant this size. Middie doesn't seem to see that . . . Yes . . . No—don't bother about changing the name, Nora. We can do all that ourselves when we get it home . . . 'Bees' Wedding'? . . . Oh, yes. I should think that must look rather good on a snake. Wait a moment, Nora—I'll ask Middie. [*To* MIDDIE] She's called her snake 'Bees' Wedding'. What do you think? Shall I tell her to take it off the snake and keep it for Mr Trench when I take him round?

MIDDIE: That'll mean we shall have to find a name to fit the snake out with.

BRO: Let's see what 'Bees' Wedding' looks like on Mr Trench, first. [*Into the telephone*] Hold on a moment, Nora.

[MIDDIE *and* BRO *look out for a few moments through the window into the garden*]

What do you think?

MIDDIE: Wait till he turns round.

BRO: Remember she's got the upstairs as well.

MIDDIE: Yes—well, it's better, anyway, than 'Mr Trench' for him.

BRO: I'll just tell her to keep 'Bees' Wedding' for Mr Trench, then.

MIDDIE: Ask her about 'Mr Trench' on the snake; see what she thinks.

BRO [*into the telephone*]: Nora? . . . Yes, it fits beautifully . . . Tailor-made, Nora . . . Would you, Nora? I was going to ask you if you wouldn't mind doing that . . . [*To* MIDDIE] She's trying it on the snake, now.

[*There is a knock at the front door.*
MIDDIE exits, closing the door behind her. BRO waits, humming to himself]

[*Into the telephone*] Oh, splendid, Nora . . . No—no trouble at all . . . That's better still . . . In about half an hour, then . . . Yes. Good-bye, Nora. [*He replaces the receiver*]

[MIDDIE *enters*]

MIDDIE: It was lucky we rang her up.

BRO: Did she say how short this snake was?

MIDDIE: She didn't give any measurements, if that's what you mean.

BRO: I thought perhaps you might have thought to ask her what the measurements were.

MIDDIE: Why didn't you ask her for the measurements yourself, as far as that goes?

BRO: How was I to know whether you'd asked already?

MIDDIE: You heard me talking to her.

[*There is a pause*]

BRO: Who was that at the door?

MIDDIE: It was two comedians. They wanted to come in and amuse us.

BRO: That's the second time this week. Where are they now?

MIDDIE: I sent them next door.

BRO: Not to Mrs Gride?

MIDDIE: I said we've already been amused, thank you.

BRO: Mrs Gride is going to be pleased—having comedians foisted on to her.

MIDDIE: She wasn't above sending the undertaker in to us, was she?

[*There is a pause*]

BRO: Were both of them funny?

MIDDIE: How should I know?

BRO: I just wondered if one was funnier than the other.

MIDDIE: They just asked if they could come in and be comic for a few minutes.

[*There is a pause*]

The last time we had them in here I was picking up jokes in the Hoover for days afterwards.

BRO: I suppose they didn't say how comic they were going to be?

MIDDIE: I didn't ask them.

[*There is a pause*]

BRO: I'm wondering if we've done the right thing about this snake of Nora's.

MIDDIE: You haven't done it yet.

BRO: What happens if it turns out to be about two inches long?

MIDDIE: You can always have them lengthened.

BRO: I know you can have them lengthened. But you don't get the thickness then. [*He crosses to the door and opens it*] What have you done with my gumboots?

MIDDIE: What do you want gumboots for to go down the

road a few doors with an elephant? Where are your other shoes?

BRO [*standing in the doorway*]: These are my other shoes I've got on.

MIDDIE: And I should come straight back with Mr Trench. We don't want Mrs Stencil asking a lot of questions.

BRO: I notice you've agreed to keep 'Mr Trench' for it now you know it's a snake.

MIDDIE: And what are you going to bring it back in? You can't trail a snake on a lead like a canary.

BRO: In any case I thought we'd settled on 'Hodge' for a name.

MIDDIE: 'Hodge' for a jackal. 'Gush' for an anaconda.

BRO: 'Admiral Benbow.'

MIDDIE: 'Hiram B. Larkspur.'

BRO: 'Playboy.'

MIDDIE: You're just thinking up names at random.

BRO: How else can I think them up?

MIDDIE: You can wait till you've seen how short it is.

[*There is a pause.* BRO *turns to go out of the door*]

BRO: I hate this job.

MIDDIE: You say that every year.

BRO: I've never had to do it before.

MIDDIE: You say it about other things.

[BRO *exits to the hall and re-enters almost at once*]

BRO: If it comes to that, how do you know it *is* an anaconda?

MIDDIE: What else would it be? We shall have the R.S.P.C.A. round while you stand there.

BRO: Good God!

[BRO *exits to the hall and shuts the door behind him*]

MIDDIE [*moving her head slowly from side to side*]: 'Admiral Benbow!'

[BRO, *after a few moments, re-enters. His coat collar is turned up. He turns it down and shakes water from his jacket, then picks up his newspaper, sits in the armchair and reads*]

You're not back already?

BRO: I'm not going in this rain.

MIDDIE: It's barely started yet.

BRO: I'm not going out in it. I haven't got a hat suitable for going out in the rain. You know that.

MIDDIE: You've got an eyeshield.

BRO: You gave it away.

MIDDIE: I don't mean the one I gave away. I mean the one you wear for tennis.

BRO: But that's to keep the sun out of my eyes.

MIDDIE: Couldn't you wear it back to front?

[*A knock is heard at the front door*]

[*She rises and moves to the door*] That would be too ingenious for you, I suppose.

[MIDDIE *exits to the hall.* BRO *reads the newspaper.*
MIDDIE *returns with an unopened telegram, which she hands to* BRO]

[*She sits on the sofa and works at the rug*] It's Uncle Ted and that motor-scooter again I expect. I shall be glad when we see the last of that craze.

BRO [*opening the telegram*]: What's he up to this time?

MIDDIE: He's probably been parking his motor-scooter on that piece of waste ground again behind Rachmaninov's Second Piano Concerto.

BRO: Who does that belong to?

MIDDIE: It doesn't belong to anybody. It's just a piece of waste ground.

BRO: Then they can't stop him parking his motor-scooter on it if it doesn't belong to anyone.

MIDDIE: I suppose they can't.

BRO [*reading the telegram*]: 'Arriving Euston twelve-ten send sandwiches.' [*He ponders*] The last time we had a telegram like this it was worded very differently.

MIDDIE: Perhaps we ought to take it back and get it seen to.

BRO: No. If they start playing about with the wording we shan't know where we are. It's in code. We should never decipher it.

MIDDIE: How can you tell whether it's in code?

BRO: There isn't any way of telling. Either it is or it isn't. This one is.

MIDDIE: Thank heaven for that, then. We can set our minds at rest.

BRO [*rising*]: Lucky I spotted it. [*He puts the telegram on the coffee-table*]

MIDDIE [*glancing through the window*]: Do you know it's stopped raining?

BRO: I'll get across to Nora's then with the elephant. [*He moves to the door*] What have you done with my gumboots?

MIDDIE: What do you want gumboots for to go down the road a few doors with an elephant? Where are your other shoes?

BRO: These are my other shoes I've got on.

MIDDIE: And I should come straight back with Mr Trench. We don't want Mrs Stencil asking a lot of questions.

BRO: I notice you've agreed to call it 'Mr Trench' now you know it's a snake.

MIDDIE: And what are you going to bring it back in? You can't trail a snake on a lead like a canary.

BRO: In any case I thought we'd settled on 'Hodge' for a name.

MIDDIE: 'Hodge' for an antelope. 'Gush' for a boa constrictor.

BRO: 'Admiral Benbow.'

MIDDIE: 'Hiram B. Larkspur.'

BRO: 'Playboy.'

MIDDIE: We've been through all this before. For goodness'

sake pull yourself together. We shall have the R.S.P.C.A. round while you stand there.

BRO: Perhaps we shall. Perhaps we shan't.

[BRO *exits.* MIDDIE *rises, goes to the fireplace, tidies the hearth and puts some coal on the fire.*
BRO *re-enters. He seems to have been thrown momentarily off balance, and speaks as though dazed*]

There was somebody at the door.

MIDDIE: Who?

BRO: I told him he'd better wait. [*He pauses*] He wants me to form a government.

MIDDIE: What does he look like?

BRO: He says he's working through the street directory.

[MIDDIE, *who has sized up the situation in her own way, quickly completes the tidying of the hearth, picks up two bottles from under the table and hands them to* BRO]

MIDDIE [*motioning towards the sideboard*]: You might do something about all these bottles. What does it look like if the Cabinet arrive suddenly?

BRO: He was wearing an old raincoat.

MIDDIE: He was very likely trying it on for size. [*She smooths the loose cover on the sofa*]

BRO: What would he be doing trying an old raincoat on for size?

MIDDIE: It might not be as old as the one he had before. [*She pauses*] The coat he had before may have been in tatters for all you or I know. It may have been black with grease.

BRO: I doubt it. I very much doubt it.

MIDDIE: Or mud or something.

BRO: Mud possibly. But not grease.

MIDDIE: Why not grease? [*She goes into the hall, leaving the door open, and is seen foraging among the coats*]

BRO: There's no grounds for thinking it's grease any more than mud. [*He takes a pipe from the mantelpiece and begins thoughtfully filling it*] How can I start forming a Government at six o'clock in the evening?

[MIDDIE *comes in holding up a torn and dirty raincoat*]

MIDDIE: Look at this thing. How do you know his mightn't have been in a worse state than this one? Look—what's that but grease? Look at the sleeves. And his was probably as bad or worse. [*She returns the coat to the hall*]

BRO: How can I start forming a Government at six o'clock in the evening?

MIDDIE [*coming into the room*]: You'd be saying the same thing if it were six o'clock in the morning. [*She closes the door, moves to the sofa and sits*]

BRO: It's the Prime Minister's job.

MIDDIE: That's one way of shelving your responsibilities, I suppose.

BRO: It's not a question of shelving anything. I just don't want the job. And in any case where would I begin forming a Government? We don't know anybody.

MIDDIE: You could make a start by asking Uncle Ted when he gets here. And in the meantime there's a man at the door waiting for your answer.

[*There is a pause*]

BRO: How do I know he isn't wanted by the police?

MIDDIE: Why should he be?

BRO: If he is we ought to turn him over.

[MIDDIE *rises and peers from behind a curtain through the window next to the door*]

MIDDIE [*coming away*]: If he's a criminal, he's in plain clothes. That's all I can say.

BRO: I'm going to turn him over and be on the safe side.

MIDDIE: You may never get another chance to form a Government.

BRO: That goes for anything I ever choose not to do.

MIDDIE: So what's it to be?

BRO [*crossing to the door*]: I'll see what he's got to say.

[BRO *exits, closing the door.* MIDDIE *works at her rug.* BRO *re-enters, goes to the armchair, picks up his newspaper and sits.* MIDDIE *waits expectantly*]

[*Casually*] It was someone having a joke.

MIDDIE: I would have recognized him through the window.

BRO: He was disguising his voice. [*He pauses, glancing through his newspaper*] He said he thought I looked like Gladstone.

MIDDIE: And did you?

BRO: That sort of thing cuts no ice with me.

MIDDIE: You should have led him on. You should have pretended to think it was eighteen sixty-eight.

BRO: It was all of a piece with his asking me to form a Government in the first place.

MIDDIE: I hope you didn't start saying, Your mission was to pacify Ireland?

BRO: It cuts no more ice with me, that sort of thing, than Gladstone would have done if I'd been Queen Victoria. And God knows there's little enough of the Empress of India about me.

MIDDIE: It would have been playing into his hands to say, Your mission was to pacify Ireland.

BRO: I know it would have been playing into his hands.

MIDDIE: I can't think why I didn't recognize him.

BRO: I've told you he was having a joke with us.

MIDDIE: I suppose he thought he could talk you round. Like last time when they had you voting for some candidate who refused to stand.

BRO: He said he was round canvassing for the Whigs.

MIDDIE: You should have let him come in for a few moments to try your overcoat on.

BRO: He'd never have got into it.

MIDDIE: Exactly.

BRO: He was broader across the shoulders than I am. He probably still is. I doubt whether he could even have worn it like a cloak.

MIDDIE: You don't see what I'm leading up to, do you?

BRO: It would have looked thoroughly ridiculous on him.

MIDDIE: I know your overcoat would have been too small for him. Of course it would have looked ridiculous. It looks ridiculous on you most of the time. But don't you see that if he'd tried it on in here, I could have seen at a glance he wasn't a man of your build? After a time I might have been able to narrow it down still further. As it is I don't know what to think. [*She pauses*] What happened about the Government? Did you agree to form one or not?

BRO: He didn't approach me any more.

MIDDIE: I see. It didn't occur to you to raise it?

BRO: I've no desire whatever to form a Government.

MIDDIE: And while you're sitting there not wanting to form a Government, he's probably next door. Asking Mrs Gride's husband.

BRO: He's very likely forgotten all about it by now.

MIDDIE: If he's forgotten all about it already, how do we know he was genuine in the first place? It could have been any old Tom, Dick or Harry asking you to form a Government. [*She pauses*] It looks to me as if you've let yourself in for something with your bland assumptions about it being someone having a joke with us.

[UNCLE TED, *a young woman, elegantly dressed, enters quietly with the obvious intention of surprising* BRO *and* MIDDIE *who continue talking, unaware of her presence. She stands waiting for one of them to look up*]

You'll be getting a man round before you know where you are with papers to prove it's eighteen sixty-eight.

BRO: But not that I'm Gladstone.

MIDDIE: If it's eighteen sixty-eight, it makes precious little difference whether you're Gladstone or not. [*She looks up, sees* UNCLE TED *and is momentarily speechless with astonishment*] Uncle Ted! [*She rises*] Why, you've changed your sex!

[UNCLE TED *strikes an attitude which invites appraisal*]

You look lovely—doesn't he, Bro? But why ever didn't you let us know?

UNCLE TED: Surely you got the telegram I sent you?

BRO: We got one—but it was in code.

UNCLE TED [*turning*]: Oh, no! What a fool of a man!

[BRO *reacts*]

No—not you, Bro. It's that idiot at the post office.

BRO: We were wondering if you were having trouble with the motor-scooter again.

UNCLE TED: I told him when I handed it in that it wasn't to go off without being decoded first.

MIDDIE: They're not very reliable.

UNCLE TED: I gave him the code number and everything. It isn't as if he had to break it down letter by letter himself or anything. So I suppose you hadn't quite expected such a change? [*She sits on the sofa*]

MIDDIE: We shall get used to it. It just seems funny calling you 'Uncle Ted'. But you must be dying for a read.

UNCLE TED: Yes, I'd love a book, Middie. I haven't opened one since I got into the train at four o'clock this morning.

[MIDDIE *goes to the bookshelves, takes out a number of books and arranges them on a tray.* BRO *sits in the armchair*]

BRO: What sort of a journey did you have this time, Uncle Ted?

UNCLE TED: The usual kind, Bro. I just got into the train, and from then onwards it was just a matter of moving in roughly the same direction practically the whole time until I got out of it at Euston.

[MIDDIE *brings the tray of books to* UNCLE TED *and puts it on the coffee-table*]

Ah, thank you, Middie.

MIDDIE: There are some nice critical essays, if you'd like one of those. Or biography. Or I've got some textbooks in the cupboard . . . ?

[UNCLE TED *rises and takes a small book*]

UNCLE TED: No—I think I'll have this book of poems, Middie. I feel as if I could really do justice to a good poem after travelling up to Euston since four o'clock this morning. Thank you, Middie. [*She sits on the arm of the sofa and reads silently and intently*]

MIDDIE [*to* BRO; *in an undertone*]: I wonder what the next craze is going to be?

BRO [*in an undertone to* MIDDIE]: Next craze?

MIDDIE: When she gets tired of her new sex.

BRO: Oh. As long as she doesn't go back to the motor-scooter.

[*There is a pause*]

MIDDIE: Perhaps we shall be able to have that conversation presently.

BRO: Which conversation?

MIDDIE: Don't you remember we promised ourselves the next time Uncle Ted came up to have a nice long conversation about the conversation we had at the Wordsworths'? When we were all talking about what we'd been talking about at the Hunters' the week before?

BRO: We had the conversation about that last time Uncle Ted was here.

MIDDIE: So we did.

[UNCLE TED *looks up from her book, closes it, and holds it out to Middie*]

BRO: Better?

[MIDDIE *takes the book and puts it on the tray*]

UNCLE TED: That was just what I wanted, Middie. I felt like some verse after that wretched stuffy compartment.

[MIDDIE *sits on the sofa.* UNCLE TED, *from where she sits, looks across the room through the window into the garden*]

So your elephant came?

MIDDIE: Yes. And look at it.

UNCLE TED: Don't you usually have a dwarf elephant? [*She crosses to the window and looks out*]

BRO: They sent us the wrong one.

UNCLE TED: What on earth for?

BRO: We shan't know till we get the measurements from them.

MIDDIE: I can see its great ears flapping about from here.

UNCLE TED: Why didn't you query the measurements when it came?

BRO: We weren't in when they came with it.

MIDDIE: What do they think we want with an elephant that size?

BRO: It's big enough for a hotel.

MIDDIE: People think you're trying to go one better than everybody else.

UNCLE TED: Never mind. It's only once a year.

BRO: Or a private school. If we had a private school, or a hotel, we might be glad of an elephant that size.

UNCLE TED: You're not calling it 'Mr Trench' again, I hope.

BRO: Why not 'Mr Trench'?

UNCLE TED: Six years running? You can't call an elephant 'Mr Trench' six years running. It looks as if you were hard up for a name to call the animal or something.

BRO: It isn't the same animal every time, you know.

MIDDIE: If it goes berserk in the night, *I'm* not getting up to it.

BRO: As far as that goes it wasn't I who wanted to call it 'Mr Trench' the year it was a giraffe.

UNCLE TED: If it's going to go berserk in the night you'd have been better off with a smaller one.

MIDDIE: I'm not getting up to it.

BRO: It was Middie's idea it would make a pleasant change to give the name to a giraffe instead of an elephant.

MIDDIE: I think we'd be better off without it.

UNCLE TED: And be without an elephant at all?

BRO: It seems a bit late now to start complaining about calling it 'Mr Trench' six years running.

MIDDIE: I think we'd be better off without an elephant. We've done nothing except bicker ever since they came with it.

UNCLE TED: You weren't in when they came with it.

MIDDIE: That's the whole point!

[*There is silence for a few moments.* BRO *glances through the window*]

BRO: Here's young Bobby coming across the garden.

MIDDIE [*with a glance through the window*]: Nora must have sent him. She'll have sent him over with the snake.

[MIDDIE *exits*]

BRO: We're exchanging the elephant with Mrs Mortice. She's letting us have her snake.

UNCLE TED: Won't she need it herself?

BRO: It's too small for her. They sent her the wrong one.

UNCLE TED: I suppose they thought they'd better deal with you both on the same footing.

BRO: They generally do their best to be fair.

UNCLE TED: If they'd sent her the right one after having sent you the wrong one it would have led to all sorts of confusion.

BRO: No. It was Mrs Mortice who got the wrong one delivered first. We were after her.

UNCLE TED: Oh.

BRO: Not that it would have been any less confusing that way, I suppose.

[MIDDIE *enters, carrying a pencil box*]

MIDDIE: That was Nora's little boy. He's brought across our boa constrictor, Uncle Ted. [*She hands the box to* UNCLE TED]

[BRO *rises to see better*]

UNCLE TED: Do I open it? [*She slides the lid open*]

BRO [*peering into the box*]: That's never a boa constrictor.

MIDDIE: Don't let it get out of its loose-box. We shall have it eavesdropping.

UNCLE TED [*closing the box and handing it to* MIDDIE]: You don't seem to be getting much for your elephant, do you?

MIDDIE: We may decide to have it lengthened. [*She puts the box on the mantelpiece*]

UNCLE TED: Yes. But of course you won't get the thickness then.

[*There is a pause*]

BRO: Was it still raining when you went to the door, Middie?

MIDDIE: There's a slight drizzle. It's not much.

BRO: I'll give it a few minutes longer. I don't suppose Nora will mind. I don't go out in the rain oftener than I need these days, Uncle Ted. My old hat isn't up to it.

UNCLE TED: That's what you're always saying, Bro. Isn't he, Middie?

MIDDIE: Hats aren't everything in this world. There are other things besides hats.

BRO: We know they aren't everything.

UNCLE TED: I daresay there are plenty of people who wouldn't mind having a hat like yours, Bro, all the same.

BRO: It isn't so much having the hats as knowing how to make the best use of them.

MIDDIE: We can't all be blessed with hats.

UNCLE TED: I suppose plenty of people do get by without hats, but it's rather silly to pretend they don't matter.

BRO: Look at Mrs Blackboy's husband and the showers he's got through in his time with that green plastic bag he carries round on his head.

MIDDIE: That's not a hat.

BRO: Or Bella for that matter.

MIDDIE: Bella overdoes it. The time she spends on millinery she could spend on something else.

UNCLE TED: She gets through the rain though.

MIDDIE: A lot of those who are supposed to have such wonderful hats go around half the time in other people's.

UNCLE TED: Why don't you weatherproof an old lampshade or something for yourself, Bro?

BRO: I'm not much of a one for millinery, Uncle Ted.

MIDDIE: That sort of thing's all right if you've got millinery in your make-up.

BRO: I've always known what I could do, and I've always known what I couldn't do. That's the reason I never became an air hostess.

MIDDIE: Bro and I prefer to leave the showers to the ones who've got the hats for it.

BRO: The older you get the less hats you seem to have.

MIDDIE: I don't want any more hats than I've got. It's very

often the people who bother least about hats who come out of it best whenever there's heavy rain.

UNCLE TED: I've never made any pretensions to hats myself, but I prefer people who've got a few hats to the ones who haven't.

MIDDIE: I can tell you someone who *has* got a good little hat on her head. You've never met Bro's niece, Uncle Ted, have you?

BRO: Oh. Myrtle.

UNCLE TED: Isn't it Myrtle who's just got through her first thunderstorm?

MIDDIE: She sailed right through it just as if she'd got a sou'wester on.

BRO: I'd like to see her have a try at a hailstorm. She's got the hat for it.

MIDDIE: Don't you put ideas into her head. We don't want her trying to do too much all at once.

BRO: Or a storm at sea.

MIDDIE: She's all right as she is.

BRO: I think that girl's got a sou'wester hidden away some-where. You watch. She'll bring it out one of these days and surprise all of us. She looks to me as if she's got her father's sou'wester.

MIDDIE: Stan never had a sou'wester in his life. It was his plastic saucer that got him where he was. Anybody would think he was a thorough-going sou'wester man the way you talk about him.

BRO: It wasn't that he didn't have a sou'wester so much as that he could never get round to putting it on.

MIDDIE: He never had one. [*To* UNCLE TED] Stan was Bro's brother in the navy, Uncle Ted. [*To* BRO] You know perfectly well he used to borrow quite shamelessly from the other men whenever there was an important storm at sea and he couldn't get by with just his plastic saucer.

UNCLE TED [*loudly*]: I'm sure that waste-paper basket of yours has possibilities, Middie.

MIDDIE: Do you like it?

UNCLE TED: It would trim up very nicely for Bro.

MIDDIE: He's had it on. Haven't you, Bro? He tried it on for size. But he won't be seen out in it.

BRO: That sort of thing's all right for the summer.

MIDDIE: Bro hates anything that he thinks makes him look younger.

BRO: I happen to have a death-wish, that's all.

UNCLE TED [*looking at her watch*]: We're going to miss the service.

MIDDIE: It's never that time already?

BRO: We shan't miss much.

MIDDIE: Uncle Ted doesn't want to miss any of it.

[BRO *switches on the radio and tunes it in*]

BRO: It may just have started.

MIDDIE: She's travelled all the way up to Euston for it since four o'clock this morning.

BRO: Sh!

[*The prayers from the radio gradually become audible. UNCLE TED listens with determined seriousness, joining in the responses from time to time. BRO and MIDDIE listen in a manner suggesting boredom half-heartedly concealed*]

PRAYER: . . . weep at the elastic as it stretches:

RESPONSE: And rejoice that it might have been otherwise.

MIDDIE [*whispering*]: We've missed the start.

BRO: Sh!

PRAYER: Let us sing because round things roll:

RESPONSE: And rejoice that it might have been otherwise.

PRAYER: Let us give praise for woodlice and for buildings sixty-nine feet three inches high:

RESPONSE: For Adam Smith's *Wealth of Nations* published in seventeen seventy-six.

PRAYER: For the fifth key from the left on the lower manual of the organ of the Church of the Ascension in the Piazza Vittorio Emanuele the Second in the town of Castelfidardo in Italy:

RESPONSE: And for bats.

PRAYER: Let us give praise for those who compile dictionaries in large, rambling buildings, for the suitably clad men and women on our commons and in our hotels, for all those who in the fullness of time will go out to meet whatever fate awaits them; for the tall, the hamfisted, the pompous; and for all men everywhere and at all times:

RESPONSE: Amen.

PRAYER: And now let us dwell upon drugs, for their effects enlighten us; upon judo and hypnosis, for their effects enlighten us; upon privation and upon loneliness, upon the heat of the sun and the silence of deserts; upon torture, upon interrogation, upon death—for their effects enlighten us:

RESPONSE: Give us light, that we may be enlightened.

PRAYER: Give us light upon the nature of our knowing; for the illusions of the sane man are not the illusions of the lunatic, and the illusions of the flagellant are not the illusions of the alcoholic, and the illusions of the delirious are not the illusions of the lovesick, and the illusions of the genius are not the illusions of the common man:

RESPONSE: Give us light, that we may be enlightened.

PRAYER: Give us light, that, sane, we may attain to a distortion more acceptable than the lunatic's and call it truth:

RESPONSE: That, sane, we may call it truth and know it to be false.

PRAYER: That, sane, we may know ourselves, and by knowing ourselves may know what it is we know:

RESPONSE: Amen.

[*There is a pause*]

MIDDIE: That was rather nice.

[*The introductory bars of 'Sweet Polly Oliver' in a metrical version are heard through the radio*]

UNCLE TED [*rising*]: This is where we stand.

[BRO *and* MIDDIE *rise.* UNCLE TED *joins softly in the hymn-like singing. As* MIDDIE *becomes aware of this, she surreptitiously draws* BRO'S *attention to it, and both suppress their amusement. When the singing ends, there is a momentary silence, and then all begin to be excessively normal by way of neutralizing their embarrassment*]

VOICE [*from the radio*]: This evening's service, from the Church of the Hypothetical Imperative in Brinkfall, was conducted by Father Gerontius.

[BRO *switches off the radio*]

MIDDIE: It's a pity we missed the first part.
BRO: At any rate we got the last part.
MIDDIE: Naturally we got it.
BRO: Why naturally?
MIDDIE: It isn't so very easy once you've switched it on to miss the last part, is it?
BRO: Not if we switched it off too soon?
UNCLE TED: We didn't miss much of it. How did you both enjoy it? I thought it was very good.
MIDDIE: It was a lot better this week. Didn't you think so, Bro? It hasn't been at all uplifting the last few weeks.
BRO: They can't expect to keep it up week after week. They ought to give it a rest for a time.
MIDDIE: Of course, I think you got more of a real, good worship, if you know what I mean, in the old days when

they weren't afraid to let themselves go with idols and things.

UNCLE TED: You're both getting jaded. If you were to come to it fresh after a few weeks without any service at all, you'd be surprised what a difference it would make. You'd be as inspired as anything by it. It's made *me* feel thoroughly uplifted, anyway.

BRO: Isn't it rather a long journey for you, though—every time you want to hear the service? Travelling up to Euston from four o'clock in the morning?

UNCLE TED: What's the alternative? It would mean having a radio down there.

BRO: I suppose it would.

UNCLE TED: Besides, I like to come up occasionally. The only trouble about that is that it's such a long journey; and if I come here it hardly leaves me time to get back. [*She looks at her watch*]

BRO: When's your train, Uncle Ted?

UNCLE TED: It leaves Euston at nine. I shall have to be off soon.

MIDDIE: Not until you've had another read. I'm not letting you go out on a miserable two stanzas. It won't take me long to get down some more books. [*She rises and goes to the bookshelves*]

UNCLE TED: Thank you, Middie—but I really oughtn't to stop for another read.

BRO [*rising*]: You're going to stay and get some prose inside you first. Don't get those down, Middie. I've got some others outside.

MIDDIE: He's got a special little store out there, for when anybody comes unexpectedly. I expect he'll bring in one of the new books on the physical nature of the universe.

[BRO *enters with three new books, and a pair of scissors*]

BRO: You've got time for a dip in one of these before you go.

108

[*He puts the books on the sideboard and, opening one of them, begins cutting out part of a page with the scissors*]

UNCLE TED: Just a paragraph, then, Bro.

MIDDIE: You won't get anything like this in the Queen's Road. Will she, Bro.

UNCLE TED: That's surely not for me, Bro? I shall never finish it in time.

BRO [*indicating with the scissors a shorter passage*]: How about that, then? You can't have anything shorter than that— it's only a paragraph.

UNCLE TED: That's fine, thanks, Bro. He was going to give me nearly half a page, Middie.

BRO: You may want some of this with it. [*He fetches a large dictionary from the bookshelf and puts it on the coffee-table*] But try it neat first of all.

MIDDIE: What's that you're offering her with it, Bro?

BRO: It's just a dictionary. She can take the edge off it, if she finds it too strong, with a definition or two.

UNCLE TED: I'll try it without first.

[BRO *hands a cutting to* UNCLE TED]

Thank you, Bro.

BRO: Do you want one, Middie?

MIDDIE: Of course I want one.

[BRO *takes two cuttings, hands one to* MIDDIE, *keeps the other for himself, then sits in the armchair*]

Well, let's hope it won't be so long next time before we see you, Uncle Ted.

[*All raise their cuttings*]

UNCLE TED: Cheers.

BRO
MIDDIE } [*together*]: Cheers.

[All read, looking up abstractedly from time to time]

UNCLE TED [*lowering her cutting*]: Well—it's certainly got a kick to it.

BRO [*raising his eyes momentarily*]: I was hoping you'd like it.

MIDDIE: You didn't find it too strong, then?

UNCLE TED: I thought it was just right, Middie.

BRO: Why should she find it too strong? It's supposed to have a bit of a bite to it.

UNCLE TED: Is it my imagination—or could I detect monosyllables in it?

BRO: Ah—I wondered if you'd spot the monosyllables. They do give it just that extra something, I think. Middie thinks they spoil it, but . . .

UNCLE TED: Oh, no—it needed just that flavouring of monosyllables to give it a tang. But you shouldn't have cut into a new book, Bro. [*She rises, and prepares to leave*]

MIDDIE: It isn't often we have the opportunity, Uncle Ted. You mustn't leave it so long next time.

BRO: You know you're very welcome to come up here for the service any time you feel you need uplifting.

UNCLE TED: I must try and get up a bit oftener. It's that awful long journey; if only there were some way of getting round that.

MIDDIE: Couldn't you make a detour?

UNCLE TED: I'd never get here, Middie. Thanks for the read, Bro—and the service. I shall have to be off.

MIDDIE: She'll miss her train.

BRO: Yes—well, good-bye, then, Uncle Ted. Have a good journey.

UNCLE TED: Good-bye, Bro.

MIDDIE: Have you got everything?

UNCLE TED: Yes, I left my cases out in the hall.

[Uncle Ted *exits, followed by* Middie, *who closes the door behind her, leaving* Bro *alone.* Bro *gets a tray of stamps, etc, from the sideboard and sits in the armchair.* Middie *re-enters*]

Bro: We forgot to ask about the motor-scooter.

Middie: She's sold it.

Bro: When did she say that?

Middie: I asked her about it in the hall. She said she'd sold it to a salesman.

[*There is a pause*]

Bro: The last time she was here she told us she'd bought it.

[*There is a pause*]

Middie: Oh—Bro. On the news this morning—I meant to tell you—they gave the figure as eight million.

Bro: No!

Middie: That was the figure they gave. He said that a normal female cod could be the mother of eight million eggs.

Bro: Not eight million!

Middie: I thought myself it seemed rather a lot.

Bro: It's irresponsibility run riot.

[*There is a pause*]

Who on earth do they hope to get to count eight million eggs?

Middie: And they're such fiddling things to count.

Bro: Not only that—it would take eight hundred thousand pairs of hands before you'd have enough fingers to count them on. You couldn't do it with less.

Middie: I don't know I'm sure.

Bro: Eight hundred thousand people to count the eggs of a single cod. It's ludicrous.

Middie: That was the figure they gave on the news.

[There is a pause]

It's Aunt Chloe's birthday next week.

BRO [*abstractedly*]: We shall have to try and think of something for her.

[There is a pause]

MIDDIE: There's a brand-new deaf-aid upstairs. We've never used it.

BRO: Aunt Chloe hasn't been deaf for years.

[There is a pause]

It's the same whatever you think of, for that matter. Either she's got it or she doesn't need it. And she certainly doesn't need a deaf-aid.

[There is a pause]

MIDDIE: Unless we were to burst a paper bag in her ear?

[There is a pause]

BRO: You wouldn't do any good with a paper bag.

[There is a pause]

We should have to get a blank cartridge and fire that.

MIDDIE: I don't think she'd really expect anything as elaborate as that.

BRO: I wasn't suggesting we should do it.

MIDDIE: It would look a bit ostentatious.

BRO: I was only saying that that would be how we should have to do it if we were going to do it at all.

MIDDIE: After all, it isn't as if it's her twenty-first.

[There is a pause]

You won't forget you've got an elephant to deliver, Bro?

BRO: No. I was just reading in the paper here—apparently

what they said at the elementary school is true about four going into twenty five times.

MIDDIE: I should want to see it first.

BRO: It's no good just dismissing it as textbook talk, Middie. It wouldn't be in the paper unless there was something in it.

MIDDIE: No, I suppose not.

[*There is a pause*]

BRO: I suppose I'd better get round to Nora's with the elephant. [*He rises, puts the tray on the sideboard and goes to the door*] Where are my gumboots?

MIDDIE: What do you want gumboots for to go down the road a few doors with an elephant? Where are your other shoes?

BRO: I'm not going without my gumboots.

MIDDIE: For goodness' sake get them on, then, and go.

[BRO *goes into the hall, picks up a pair of gumboots and comes into the room*]

BRO: If you switch on the radio while I'm out you can listen to the play. [*He sits on the arm of the armchair, takes off his shoes and puts on the gumboots*]

MIDDIE: How long are you going to be?

BRO: You'll get the last half-hour or so of it. I don't know how long I shall be—it depends whether I meet Mrs Stencil on the way.

MIDDIE: For goodness' sake go the other way then. We don't want Mrs Stencil asking a lot of questions.

BRO: She won't be out at this time.

MIDDIE: This is just when she will be out. She always goes out in the evening exercising her butterflies.

BRO: I thought they were in quarantine?

MIDDIE: They came out of quarantine weeks ago. She's had the vet to them since then.

BRO: Well—if I meet her, I meet her.

MIDDIE: Try not to let her see the elephant.

BRO: I certainly shan't draw attention to it. [*He stands in the open doorway*] You'd better get up to bed if I'm late.

MIDDIE: *Up* to bed? I thought we were living in a bungalow?

[BRO *looks bewilderedly around, then exits to the hall closing the door behind him.* MIDDIE *leans over to the radio, switches it on, then works on her rug-making.* BRO'S *and* MIDDIE'S *voices are heard through the radio*]

BRO'S VOICE: It was your idea it would make a pleasant change to give the name to a sea-lion instead of a dinosaur.

MIDDIE'S VOICE: We've done nothing except bicker since they came with it.

[*The telephone rings*]

BRO'S VOICE: We weren't in when they came with it.

[MIDDIE *rises*]

MIDDIE'S VOICE: That's the whole point.

[MIDDIE *switches off the radio, crosses to the telephone and lifts the receiver*]

MIDDIE [*into the telephone*]: Mrs Paradock . . . Oh, Mrs Stencil . . . Yes . . . No, Bro's just this moment gone out . . . Yes . . . Yes . . . Yes, I can imagine . . . Of course it is . . . Of course . . . Yes . . . Yes . . . Oh, but I think they get used to it, Mrs Stencil, don't they? . . . They get a sort of head for heights . . . I really don't think heights worry them, Mrs Stencil . . . Some birds, perhaps—but not eagles . . . Oh, yes. Eagles do . . . Yes . . . But it must be very rare, however high they fly . . . It must be very rare for an eagle to come over dizzy . . . Yes . . . Yes . . . But wouldn't that give them the feeling of being rather hampered? . . . Yes . . . But I do think an eagle likes to swoop down sometimes . . . But not if it's wearing a parachute . . . Oh, I can understand how you feel, Mrs Stencil . . . Yes . . . Yes . . . [*Hesitantly*] I'm afraid it would have to be more or less a token subscription this time—this is always our expensive quarter . . . No, naturally . . . No . . . Anyway, I'll tell Bro when he comes in, and . . . Yes . . . Yes . . . I suppose they must . . . It's the peering down, I expect . . . Yes . . . They must be peering down most of the time . . . And of course with some of them they're supposed to stare into the sun as well, aren't they? . . . Don't eagles stare at the sun? . . . Yes . . . Still, I should think if they found that . . . Yes . . . But if they found it was becoming a strain on their eyes they'd surely stop doing it . . . Yes . . . But I doubt whether they'd take the trouble to wear them once the novelty had worn off . . . Oh, they are—they're very expensive. Even the steel-rimmed ones . . . Yes . . . Yes . . . A kind of Welfare State for animals, in fact . . . Yes—well, I'll tell Bro, Mrs Stencil, when he comes in and . . . Yes . . . Yes, I will, Mrs Stencil . . . Good-bye. [*She replaces the receiver, switches on the radio, then sits on the sofa*]

[BRO's *and* MIDDIE's VOICES *are heard through the radio*]

MIDDIE's VOICE: What do you want gumboots for to go down the road a few doors with a dinosaur? Where are your other shoes?

BRO's VOICE: I'm not going without my gumboots.

MIDDIE's VOICE: For goodness' sake get them on, then, and go.

[BRO *enters, wearing his gumboots. The voices on the radio give way to interval music.* BRO *closes the door, sits in the armchair and takes off his gumboots*]

MIDDIE: You didn't stay at Nora's long. [*She switches off the radio*]

BRO: I didn't stay at Nora's at all. Where are my slippers?

MIDDIE: Mrs Stencil rang up.

BRO [*putting on his shoes*]: Oh? What is it this time? Emergency breathing apparatus for deep-sea fish again?

MIDDIE: Apparently she's still on the Appeals Committee for the Birds of Prey Protection League.

BRO: I'm not putting my hand in my pocket every few weeks for that. And you can tell her I said so. Birds of prey! They're just as capable of looking after themselves as we are.

MIDDIE: That's what I said to Mrs Stencil. Besides, what do eagles want with parachutes?

BRO: Is that what she's collecting for?

MIDDIE: Or any other bird for that matter. She's got it into her head they need to have some kind of safety equipment.

BRO: They've got their two wings, haven't they?

MIDDIE: Mrs Stencil's worried what would happen if they were to get cramp or anything while they were up there.

BRO: She fusses.

MIDDIE: I think she's hoping that if the League can provide a few parachutes out of their own funds, she might be able . . .

BRO: Out of *our* funds.

MIDDIE: She's hoping she might get the authorities interested in supplying spectacles for them.

BRO: For whom?

MIDDIE: For the eagles and things. I told her I didn't think many of them would bother wearing glasses once the novelty had worn off.

[*There is a pause.* BRO *picks up his newspaper and reads*]

It's the height they have to peer down from before they swoop. She thinks it puts too much strain on their eyes.

BRO: They don't have to peer down. They're free agents.

MIDDIE: That's what I said to her.

BRO: Parachutes. Glasses. They get too much done for them.

[*There is a pause*]

Was that the play you were listening to when I came in?

MIDDIE: You didn't want it, did you? I switched it off.

BRO: We may as well see how it ends.

[MIDDIE *switches on the radio and takes up her rug.* BRO *continues to be occupied with the newspaper.* MIDDIE'S *and* BRO'S *voices are heard through the radio*]

MIDDIE'S VOICE: And what did Edna say?

BRO'S VOICE: I didn't get as far as Edna's.

MIDDIE'S VOICE: Where have you been, then?

BRO'S VOICE: I've been in the garden.

MIDDIE'S VOICE: Not all the time? [*She pauses*] In the garden doing what?

BRO'S VOICE [*exasperated*]: In the garden trying to get that blasted dinosaur through the gate!

MIDDIE'S VOICE: Really! [*She pauses*] I'm going out to make a drink for myself. [*She pauses*] What are *you* having—coffee? Or cocoa?

BRO'S VOICE: Hot milk.

[*The interval music is heard again.* MIDDIE *switches off the radio*]

BRO [*gloomily*]: What was the rest of it like?

MIDDIE: You didn't miss much.

[MIDDIE *takes up her rug.* BRO *reads. A long silence intervenes*]

And what did Nora say?

BRO: I didn't get as far as Nora's.

MIDDIE: You've been out there for hours. What have you been doing?

BRO: I've been in the garden.

MIDDIE: Not all the time?

BRO: I was out there for less than twenty minutes and I

shouldn't have met with any more success if I'd been out there all night.

MIDDIE: I don't know what you're talking about.

BRO: I'm talking about that bloody elephant!

MIDDIE: Bro!

BRO: How do you expect me or anybody else to get a whacking great oaf of an elephant through a gate wide enough to take a pram?

[MIDDIE *puts down her rug and is about to go, tight-lipped, to the door*]

MIDDIE [*rising; conclusively*]: It was got *in*. [*She moves to the door*] What are you having to drink? Cocoa? Or coffee?

[MIDDIE *pauses at the door, and turns in the act of going out as she waits in tightly reined impatience for* BRO'S *answer.* BRO *is still under the influence of his own irritation, so that some seconds pass before he registers* MIDDIE'S *question. When he does so, he reflects for a moment before answering*]

BRO: Hot milk.

CURTAIN

Barnstable

by

JAMES SAUNDERS

First broadcast on 20 November 1959 on the
B.B.C. Third Programme. Producer, Donald McWhinnie

First performed at the Questors Theatre, Ealing,
on 13 June 1960

Cast

HELEN CARBOY
CHARLES CARBOY
REV. WANDSWORTH TEETER
DAPHNE CARBOY
SANDRA

Barnstable

THE SCENE: *A drawing-room, lit by the morning sun which streams through the french windows facing on to the lawn. At them, looking out, stands* HELEN CARBOY, *wrapped in thought. Two thrushes sing.* HELEN CARBOY *looks up at the sky. There is the sound of a shot. One of the thrushes continues to sing. Another shot, and the thrush falls silent.*

HELEN: Oh, God . . .

> [*A moment's pause, and the door opens.* CHARLES CARBOY, *her father, and the* REV. WANDSWORTH TEETER, *enter*]

CARBOY: . . . It's not right, you know, and it worries me. Nothing you could put your finger on, you understand, I couldn't give a diagnosis; in fact to be quite honest I'm not even sure about the symptoms. But I'm convinced it's not as it should be.

TEETER: Well, well . . .

CARBOY: That's all very fine, but you're not personally involved. You're just a bystander.

> [HELEN *turns impulsively and goes to the telephone. She lifts the receiver and dials.* CARBOY *is in plus fours, and unremarkable, neither portly nor slim, looking as though chronic indigestion suits him well.* TEETER *is collared.* CARBOY *carries a dead mole by the tail, which he drops in the course of the conversation on to a copy of* The Spectator *on the same*

occasional table at the other side of which HELEN *is at the telephone, though they ignore each other*]

TEETER: Charles, my heart bleeds . . .

CARBOY: Now, now, Wandsworth, I don't blame you. Why *should* you let it trouble you? I know the feeling; I feel precisely the same when *I'm* in somebody else's garden. I say to myself: there's some Stratiotes Sylvaticus growing over there; and that's an end to it. Not a thought to the health of the thing, not a thought to its owner, who nurtures it. So I appreciate your point of view, you see.

HELEN: I wish to emigrate.

CARBOY: But at the same time you must realize that while to you this is just somebody else's Stratiotes Sylvaticus, to me it's *my* Stratiotes Sylvaticus, growing in *my* garden. You try saying well well in a case like that. The boot's on the other foot.

HELEN: I *am* holding on.

TEETER: I'm sure it'll all turn out for the best.

CARBOY: Ah, but will it?

TEETER: My dear Charles . . .

CARBOY: You're an idealist, Wandsworth, if I may say so, but I'm a realist. I face facts. I look the situation in the eye. And the way I see it is this: the soil's right, the acidity's right, I've had it checked, there's no doubt about the acidity. It's had a nice mild winter . . .

[HELEN *is jiggling the receiver rest*]

. . . I've cl*oched it, I've watered it, I've sprayed it. It's against the south wall, nicely protected. And yet it's not well. There's something the matter with it. It's not well . . .

HELEN: Hallo. Will you please speak!

CARBOY: . . . And we don't know why. Well, then, perhaps it'll get better, as you say; but I don't see why it should. Why should it? I tell you, quite honestly, I'm worried about that Stratiotes Sylvaticus.

HELEN: Yes, emigrate, emigrate!

TEETER: I wish I could advise you. A message of hope is all I can offer . . .

HELEN: How far can one go?

CARBOY: I shouldn't burden you with my problems . . .

TEETER: No, no. What are old friends for?

HELEN: New Zealand? Is that the farthest?

TEETER: Could it perhaps be the air?

CARBOY: In what way?

TEETER: It's just a thought. You say the soil's right and the treatment's right and the aspect's right. All that's left really is the air . . .

HELEN: Yes, yes, further than that!

CARBOY [*after a moment's thought*]: The *air* . . . now that's a new line of approach certainly . . .

HELEN: Fiji is useless! Further, further!

TEETER: Something in the air perhaps . . .

HELEN: Is there nowhere unknown, is there nowhere . . . ?

CARBOY: Which . . .

TEETER: Tends to, perhaps . . .

HELEN [*putting down the receiver*]: It doesn't matter . . .

CARBOY: But it was all right last year. I tell you, the soil's right, the acidity's right . . .

HELEN [*with a sob*]: Oh, God!

[*The two men turn to look at her*]

TEETER: My dear Miss Carboy . . .

HELEN: I'm terribly sorry, it's most idiotic of me. I don't know what has come over me. It's really most frightfully idiotic of me, I'm really most frightfully sorry . . . .I must write a letter. [*She goes out*]

CARBOY: It had a nice mild winter. It's sheltered from the wind . . .

TEETER: Is something troubling Helen?

CARBOY: Who?

TEETER: Your daughter is not herself.

CARBOY: I believe she's worried about young Bob.

TEETER: Young Bob, eh?

CARBOY: You know young Bob?

TEETER: I know *a* young Bob. Whether the same one . . .

CARBOY: The same, the same . . . Her brother . . .

TEETER: Tck tck tck.

CARBOY: Well, well . . .

[*A pause*]

And now moles under the lawn. [*He indicates the body*] What can one do?

TEETER: Young Bob, eh?

CARBOY: I'll get some of the air in the garden analysed, of course, but I don't see what good it'll do . . .

TEETER: Well, well . . . The Lord giveth and the Lord taketh away . . .

CARBOY: What *does* one do about moles?

TEETER: Block up their burrows?

CARBOY: Where there's one mole there'll be another.

TEETER: Or arsenic . . .

CARBOY: And how does one get the air into the bottle?

[DAPHNE CARBOY *tries to enter the french windows. Finding rattling useless, she kicks at the door. Her first two kicks hit the door, but the third puts her foot through one of the lower panes of glass*]

TEETER: I believe Daphne wants to come in.

CARBOY: Who?

TEETER: Your wife.

CARBOY: I'm worried about this mole, you know. [*As he talks he goes to the french windows and attempts to open them*]

TEETER: This one?

CARBOY: I mean its implications. Greenfly is one thing; but when things . . . start coming up at you . . . from under the ground . . . it's something else again. [*He stops trying for a moment*] At least worms are discreet about it.

TEETER: They are all God's creatures.

CARBOY: Well now, I don't want to lay the blame anywhere. I just want them out . . . from under my . . . lawn.

[*With the last word he manages to wrench open the windows. DAPHNE CARBOY comes in*]

DAPHNE: Charles, I'm worried about Helen.

CARBOY: Yes, dear . . .

DAPHNE: Wandsworth, how nice to see you so early. Have you met my husband?

CARBOY: Twenty years ago!

DAPHNE: Really, as long ago as that?

CARBOY [*embarrassed*]: It's always the same, these sunny mornings.

DAPHNE: How old was I then?

CARBOY: It's immaterial!

DAPHNE: Oh, my poor dear dead husband . . .

TEETER: Yes, well, yes, well . . .

[*He coughs and looks out of the french windows. CARBOY goes to the table and swings the dead mole nervously by the tail*]

DAPHNE: Things were different then. [*She looks from one to the other for confirmation, but they avoid her eyes*] Roseate, it was. Halcyon. When my poor dear husband used to take me by the hand down into the rose garden, and there we'd sit, with the scent of the roses heavy in the air and our faces rosy with the setting sun. There we'd sit without a word till the roses lost their colour and the last light went from the sky . . . [*She sobs discreetly*]

CARBOY: It was me.

DAPHNE: Who's that?

CARBOY: I was your husband. You've only had one husband. Every spring we have this.

DAPHNE: There was another, I'm sure of it.

CARBOY: We have enough on our plate as it is. Look at this.

DAPHNE: A vole?

CARBOY: Not a vole, a *mole*.

DAPHNE: Dead?

CARBOY: Would I be holding it by the tail if it were not?

DAPHNE: One holds rabbits by the ears, what do you expect of me? So now he's taken to shooting moles . . .

CARBOY: Who?

DAPHNE: Barnstable. Who else would shoot moles?

CARBOY: Nonsense, dear. I killed this mole.

DAPHNE: *You* shot it?

CARBOY: Not shot. I hit it with a spade.

DAPHNE: I heard a shot.

CARBOY: How could there be a shot when I hit it with a spade?

DAPHNE: There was a shot.

CARBOY: I heard no shot. You imagined a shot. It was a bird.

DAPHNE: A bird shot?

CARBOY: Not shot! The shot was a bird. Or the wind. Something.

DAPHNE: Shooting of defenceless moles . . .

CARBOY: Not moles! Not moles!

DAPHNE: It comes to the same. Two shots rang out, say what you like. If it wasn't a mole it was something else.

[*There is a pause.* DAPHNE *drops her flowers on to the table, takes a pair of secateurs from her pocket and begins to cut their stems*]

CARBOY: You cut flowers. You think nothing of that. You cut them down in their prime. A flower is a flower. Very well, then. If you shot them it would come to the same . . .

[DAPHNE *ignores him: he loses interest in the argument and stands swinging the mole idly.* TEETER *turns from the windows*]

TEETER: In the midst of one's adversities one should remember one is not alone. Others, too, have had their tribulations . . .

There was a garden in Hackney Wick where the Stratiotes Sylvaticus was never up to standard. He was a God-fearing man, but from one year to the next his Stratiotes Sylvaticus was a disappointment.

CARBOY: The soil was wrong, but in *my* case . . .

TEETER: Ah, now, but that is the surprising thing about it; one day the police came and dug up his Stratiotes Sylvaticus

CARBOY: The police?

TEETER: And discovered that his *wife* . . . was underneath them all the time!

CARBOY: Well, there you are.

TEETER: Perhaps. But this is the enigma: whether it was his wife's complaining about the state of them which caused him to put her underneath them; or whether his putting her underneath them caused them to lose the will to live.

CARBOY: A sprinkling of bonemeal is all they need. A sprinkling. Mine have had that. But they're not right.

TEETER: God's will be done.

CARBOY: That's all very well.

DAPHNE: I am worried about which vase to put these flowers in. Many small vases, or one large.

[*The telephone rings.* CARBOY *answers it*]

CARBOY: Yes . . . No, no, no. Now listen carefully: take *three* of the small red pills twice a day followed by *four* of the large blue pills three times a day . . . In water, in water; and the liniment at blood-heat. Is that clear? . . . Being colour-blind is irrelevant. The red pills are small, the large pills are blue . . . The white pills are for emergencies. I'll call on Tuesday, if you're still with us. [*He replaces the receiver*]

TEETER: One wonders that a mole bothers to have a tail at all, it can only be an inconvenience.

CARBOY: She has rubbed the pills on her chest and drunk the liniment. And she's getting better. What do they expect of one . . .?

TEETER: You should take a day off occasionally.

CARBOY: I do. It makes no difference. The mortality rate is the same.

TEETER: Yes, I see that. But if you were to take a day off occasionally . . .

DAPHNE: Charles.

CARBOY: One large vase. In water three times a day.

DAPHNE: Charles, I'm worried about Helen.

CARBOY: Yes, yes . . .

DAPHNE: Not only that, but I'm also worried about Barnstable.

[CARBOY *looks up*. TEETER *coughs*]

In fact I'm worried about Barnstable more than I'm worried about Helen.

[SANDRA, *the maid, comes in*]

CARBOY: What is it, Sandra?

SANDRA [*soundlessly*]: If you please, I'm giving notice.

CARBOY: Speak up, speak up.

SANDRA: If you please, I'm giving notice.

CARBOY: Nonsense. You may go.

SANDRA [*soundlessly*]: I'm sorry.

CARBOY: What?

SANDRA: I'm sorry . . .

CARBOY: Nonsense! [*He holds up his mole by the tail and speaks to it*] She comes in here without a by-your-leave and says she's giving *notice*. [*He turns to* SANDRA] You seem to forget what you are. I've a good mind to give you notice.

SANDRA: Oh, sir . . .

CARBOY: What do you make of it, Wandsworth?

TEETER: Let us not be precipitate. Come here, my child.

[SANDRA *goes up to him*]

You may speak freely to me. Are you not happy here?

SANDRA: It's the thrushes, sir.

TEETER: You don't like thrushes?

SANDRA: Last week it was squirrels. Now it's thrushes.

TEETER: What is, my child?

SANDRA: Shot, sir.

CARBOY: Nonsense!

TEETER: Hush . . . Not here, Sandra. Not in this country. You have imagined it all.

SANDRA: They're out there on the lawn.

TEETER: No, no. Imagined, imagined. Fulfil your tasks diligently, Sandra. Girdle your horizons with honest toil. There, you feel better already. Don't you?

SANDRA: I don't know, sir.

TEETER: Come to me when you are in trouble. I am an open door.

SANDRA: Yes, sir.

CARBOY: You may go.

SANDRA: What shall I do about the thrushes on the lawn, sir?

CARBOY: Let them lie.

SANDRA: Yes, sir. [*She is going out*]

TEETER: Sandra.

SANDRA: Yes, sir.

TEETER: Do you ever speak to strangers?

SANDRA: Not unless I know them, sir.

TEETER: If you should, and they should tell you things . . .

SANDRA: Oh, sir.

TEETER: Believe them not.

SANDRA: Yes, sir.

TEETER: All is as it seems. Let that be your golden thought. Carry it with you like a banner. All is as it seems.

SANDRA: Yes, sir.

TEETER: Birds, too, have their resting place, their haven.

SANDRA: Yes, sir.

TEETER: You may go.

SANDRA: Yes, sir.

CARBOY: And let it not occur again.

SANDRA: No, sir. [*She is going*]

DAPHNE: Sandra.

SANDRA: Yes, madam.

DAPHNE: Bring me a vase. One large vase.

SANDRA: Yes, ma'am. [*She goes out*]

TEETER: Tck tck tck tck tck tck . . .

CARBOY: No taste; no tact.

TEETER: Nearer the earth, of course . . .

CARBOY: It's ingrained in them.

TEETER: She does her best, perhaps . . .

CARBOY: That's not the point.

TEETER: Well, no . . .

[*There is a pause*]

DAPHNE: So it's thrushes now.

CARBOY: What?

DAPHNE: Sandra is right. Last week it was squirrels. This week it's thrushes. Where's it all going to end?

CARBOY: Thrushes, squirrels, it makes no difference.

DAPHNE: It seems hard . . .

CARBOY: The thrushes must look after themselves. The world is what it is.

TEETER: One should, moreover, bear this in mind: man is but a grain of sand in the desert. The desert has its reason and its purpose, but what does the grain of sand know of that, parched and trodden underfoot by the pads of itinerant camels? There is a benevolence all unbeknownst. The thrush falls; why? Who can tell? Reason, purpose, nevertheless, must there be. The chafing babe cries, but maternal wisdom presides . . . We chafe, we fret, we question; only the mind-blind bird, unquestioning, blissful sings . . .

[*There is a shot. The mind-blind bird gives up singing*]

DAPHNE: Another.

TEETER: And I must go.

CARBOY: So soon?

TEETER: I must keep moving. To spread comfort.

DAPHNE: You are a good man.

TEETER: Life must go on. [*He goes out through the french windows*]

DAPHNE: He is such a comfort.

CARBOY: I'm worried about the Stratiotes Sylvaticus. And the moles.

DAPHNE: I'm worried about Helen and young Bob.

CARBOY: I'm worried about old Mrs Fagoty. If she loses her head and takes the white pills she's done for. And I'm worried about the moles.

DAPHNE: I'm worried about Charles, he worries too much.

CARBOY: I'm worried about the lease of the house.

DAPHNE: I'm worried about that vase.

CARBOY: Only another forty-three years, and then what? It just goes to show, one should never take out a ninety-nine-year lease. A *nine hundred* and ninety-nine-year lease, now, there's *stability*. Well, well, we shall know next time ...

DAPHNE: I'm worried about Sandra.

CARBOY: I'm worried about whether to clean my teeth before shaving and then wash, or wash before cleaning my teeth and then shave, and I'm worried about whether to wear my shirt-tail outside my underpants for comfort or inside my underpants for security.

DAPHNE: I'm worried about Helen.

CARBOY: I'm worried about old Mrs Fagoty. Should I ring her up? After all, she's seventy-eight.

DAPHNE: And the vase.

CARBOY: I'm worried about whether to ring her up.

DAPHNE: And Helen and Sandra.

CARBOY: If only she weren't on the phone. Why did I ever give her the white pills in the first place? I must have been mad. It isn't as though she needs the pills. Red, white and blue pills, she could do without the lot. And the liniment. There's nothing wrong with her that old age won't cure.

As long as she doesn't take the pills. If she died tomorrow nobody would mind, least of all old Mrs Fagoty. Unless she dies of the white pills. Then some busybody will come and look inside her stomach. Find it chockful of white pills . . . Ask me why I *gave* her the white pills . . . I don't know why I gave her the white pills. I don't even remember what she was suffering from, apart from living. Insomnia, pains in the . . . shoulder, I haven't the faintest idea. What was *in* the white pills? I don't know. Maybe she'll leave them in the kitchen and the cat will get them. One can but hope. What they'll do to her cat is not my business. I'm no vet. Turn it into a dog, perhaps. Or is it a dog she has already? It's called Agamemnon, that I remember. Would that be a cat or a dog? Dear God, let old Mrs Fagoty die of old age . . .

DAPHNE: And Barnstable. And Barnstable. And Barnstable . . .

CARBOY [*exasperated*]: My dear Daphne, here we are with moles under our very lawn and you . . .

[*There is a long, sad rumbling sound, culminating in a crash. A piece of plaster falls from the ceiling*]

DAPHNE: There!

CARBOY: I don't follow your reasoning.

DAPHNE: Another chimney falling. It's all this shooting.

CARBOY: Not necessarily . . .

DAPHNE: Do you deny it?

CARBOY: One must look at both sides of the question.

DAPHNE: Ever since the shooting started chimneys have been falling.

CARBOY: Chimneys have always been falling. The week we arrived a chimney fell. They've been falling ever since. It's a law of nature. Depreciation. What can one expect?

DAPHNE: But not so frequently.

CARBOY: When he used to stamp to and fro in his boots you said that was making the chimneys fall; now he shoots thrushes you say that makes the chimneys fall. It needs nothing . . . Chimneys fall. It's a law of nature. That's all there is to it. They stand up and then after a time they fall down. Depreciation. What do you expect of a chimney? Chimneys are only human, like the rest of us.

DAPHNE: Last week a shot rang out and then a chimney fell.

CARBOY: Not at all. On the contrary. Your memory is at fault, Daphne. A: you say a shot rang out and then a chimney fell. On the contrary a chimney fell and then a shot rang out. B: it was not a chimney at all. You *said* it was a chimney, just as you thought it fell after the shot rang out whereas in *fact*, on the contrary, it fell before the shot rang out and it was not a chimney at all but the roof of the west wing. If you will cast your mind back . . .

DAPHNE: Are you suggesting that it was the roof of the west wing falling in which caused the shot to ring out?

CARBOY: Not at all. Neither am I saying that it is my Stratiotes Sylvaticus which is causing the moles to burrow under the lawn.

DAPHNE: Moles always burrow under lawns. It's a law of nature.

CARBOY: Exactly. The crux of my argument.

DAPHNE: Oh . . .

CARBOY: And chimneys have to fall.

DAPHNE: But not so frequently.

CARBOY: Yes, yes, as frequently. It's a law of nature . . . In any case you were wrong once, you may be wrong again. You say it's a chimney. How do you know it's a chimney?

DAPHNE: It sounded like a chimney.

CARBOY: When the roof of the west wing fell in you said it sounded like a chimney. It was a roof nevertheless. This may be a chimney. But it may be a roof. We don't know, Daphne, we just don't know. Let us be realistic.

DAPHNE: It sounded more like a chimney than a roof to me.

CARBOY: When the roof of the west wing fell in you said . . .

[*There is another long, sad rumbling sound, culminating in a crash. A piece of plaster falls from the ceiling*]

DAPHNE: There! Another!

CARBOY: There's no arguing with you.

DAPHNE: It's Barnstable, Barnstable!

CARBOY: Not necessarily.

[HELEN *comes in.* DAPHNE *begins to arrange her flowers on the table.* CARBOY *picks up the mole*]

HELEN: I wish to apologize for making an exhibition of myself.

DAPHNE: What, dear?

HELEN: Father, I wish to apologize for making an.. . .

CARBOY: Yes, yes. Life's full enough as it is . . .

HELEN: It was absolutely idiotic of me. I don't know how I can ever forgive myself for being so absolutely idiotic.

CARBOY: It's over and done with . . .

HELEN: And fatuous.

[CARBOY *shrugs his shoulders in embarrassment*]

And inane, absolutely fatuous and inane. I feel absolutely idiotic. I don't know what Wandsworth Teeter must have thought of me.

CARBOY: Nothing, nothing.

HELEN: He must have thought me absolutely fatuous and inane and idiotic. After all, he is so absolutely marvellous and good . . .

[*There is a silence*]

He's so absolutely mature and sensible and kind. I feel as though I could crawl under his feet, he's so good and so kind and I made an absolutely fatuous exhibition of myself . . .

[CARBOY *swings the mole frantically.* DAPHNE *looks on in bewilderment.* HELEN *goes to the french windows*]

The sun is shining straight down on to the garden.

CARBOY: The grass isn't ready for it yet.
HELEN: Just as though nothing will happen.

[*There is a pause*]

Harold has asked me to go out riding with Peggy and Oscar this afternoon, to meet Cyril and Betty and then play squash at Robin's; but Robin is playing croquet at David's with Meryl and Cedric, and Cecil can't come because of his cousin Agnes who's a bad sailor; but if I go boating with Mervyn and Gilbert they'll bring Rosemary and Perkin, and he'll bring Humphrey and Leslie and Lavinia and Claire, and Claire will bring Timothy and Elspeth. If only I had a real *friend*: they are all so . . . idiotic. Fatuous, terribly inane, I feel so idiotically lonely and inane and inane and Wandsworth Teeter is so big and so strong and so kind and so terribly . . . *understanding*, the sun is shining all over the lawn, is there going to be a storm or something terrible or what, oh God! Mother, I'm worried about Ernest.

DAPHNE: Ernest, dear?
HELEN: He has asked me to marry him.
DAPHNE: What, after you've been engaged to him for five years?
HELEN: Why can't people accept things as they are?
CARBOY: It's the thin end of the wedge. He gets engaged and the next minute he wants to get married. He'll be setting up house with you next, mark my words.
HELEN: It's so terribly humiliating and . . . *degrading*.
CARBOY: And share his meals with you. It'll come to that.
HELEN: Why is everything so terribly involved and . . . and . . . *sordid*? Once he touched my hand with his finger. I felt utterly humiliated and wretched. I lay on my bed for three days staring at the ceiling and feeling utterly humiliated and . . . and . . . *unclean*. There are dead thrushes all over the lawn. And the roof of the east wing has fallen in.

CARBOY: Nonsense.

HELEN: It's true. I saw it fall.

DAPHNE: Well, well, it'll put itself right again, I daresay.

CARBOY: Things are never as bad as they seem.

HELEN: If only I could stop thinking. Father, I think there is somebody living upstairs.

CARBOY: What?

DAPHNE: Hush, dear.

HELEN: I've heard his footsteps! *He* shoots the thrushes.

CARBOY: Nonsense, nonsense!

DAPHNE: How could there be, dear . . . ?

CARBOY: Exactly. How could there be anyone living upstairs . . . when there *aren't any stairs*? There are *moles* on the lawn. The lawn is covered with moles. You mistook them for thrushes. It's perfectly obvious. Here is the proof. [*He holds up the mole*]

DAPHNE: Now why don't you have a nice cup of cocoa and go to bed?

HELEN: How can I go to bed when the roof has fallen on to my bedroom?

DAPHNE: Shall we have a game of ludo together?

HELEN: No, no . . . Perhaps I shall drive into town with Malcolm. Only he's incomprehensible. What shall I do? Shall I stay home and write inane letters to people I despise? Shall I pick flowers . . .?

DAPHNE: No more flowers, we're swamped as it is.

HELEN: Sometimes I think I shall go mad, mad. If only I could. Mother, am I going mad, is that it?

CARBOY: When I was a boy I loved nothing better than to sleep on the roof in fine weather. Now, wait . . . If I were to bury hypodermic needles all over the lawn, that would give them something to think about.

HELEN: Something is going to happen, something absolutely inane and dreadful is going to happen, what shall I do? There's a sort of impending doom. Shall I fish, shall I pick

flowers? Shall I paint water-colours in the garden . . .?
What do I know that no one else knows . . .?

[*There is a crash*]

DAPHNE: Well, *that* was a chimney-pot, come what may.

[SANDRA *comes in. She is wheeling a trolley on which is an enormous vase*]

SANDRA [*soundlessly*]: If you please, sir . . .
CARBOY: Speak up, my girl.
SANDRA: If you please, sir, the east wing has fallen.
CARBOY: Nonsense, nonsense! Learn your place, my girl.
DAPHNE: Bring it over here, Sandra.

[SANDRA *does so*]

You may pick flowers now, Helen. As many as you like.
Pick *all* the flowers. We shall arrange a centrepiece for the
dining-room.
SANDRA: The dining-room's gone, ma'am.
CARBOY: Gone?
SANDRA: Fallen, sir.
CARBOY: Nonsense, nonsense! It's all these paperbacks, that's
the cause of it. Apply yourself, my girl. Be diligent. Cast
your eye downwards. Humility. Sacrifice. How dare you!
Remember your place!

[*There is a crash. Plaster*]

DAPHNE: More frequently.
SANDRA: Oh, sir . . .
CARBOY: Nonsense. It was nothing. A bird falling. Let us at
all events keep calm.
HELEN: It's coming . . . Shall I read a book? Shall I attempt a
potato-cut? Shall I knit an Alpine pullover? [*She turns to the
room, speaking hysterically*] I wish to give notice that I
hereby disclaim responsibility for all debts incurred by
members of my family . . .

137

[There is a tremendous crash. A large gilt-framed portrait of a Caroline drinking party falls to the floor. The lights go out]

SANDRA: Sir, I wish to give notice!

CARBOY: Keep calm, kindly keep calm!

[There is a pause. CARBOY strikes a match]

Let us keep our heads. My assessment of the situation is this: the sun appears to have gone temporarily out. That is all. I have no doubt that it will be remedied in due course of time . . . *[His match goes out]* Meanwhile we must do the best we can to behave as Englishmen.

DAPHNE: Should we perhaps switch *our* lights on?

CARBOY: No, no. Better not to meddle with the course of nature. One doesn't burn electricity in broad daylight . . .

[There is a pause. SANDRA sobs]

Be quiet, my girl. Learn your place . . . To be English is everything . . . When I was in the trenches, in 1915, my imperturbability was a byword. The men had a nickname for me, I remember; they used to call me Imperturbable Robinson . . . Why Robinson I never discovered . . . I was, though I say it, an inspiration to the men. Men, I used to say to them as we waited for the signal to advance—men, in another moment we shall be advancing upon the enemy through a hail of machine-gun bullets. We shall be enfiladed from the right, enfiladed from the left, and bombarded by mortars from the centre. In the event of our succeeding in crossing nomansland, we shall find ourselves face to face with enemy bayonets of extreme numerical superiority. Supposing us to have overcome the enemy and taken up position in their own trenches, we shall doubtless find them no less waterlogged than our own. The only apparent difference will be our greater proximity to the enemy howitzers, which will of course bombard our new-won position. However, let us not lose our sense of proportion . . .

[*There is a crash of falling masonry*]

Let us achieve a balanced judgment in the light of an all-round assessment of the situation . . .

[*His last words are drowned by another crash*]

. . . bearing in mind our mental limitations.

[*There is another crash, and a scream cut short*]

My subaltern once told me he would rather be blown up under me than under any other commanding officer. As indeed he was . . .

[*The sun comes out again. The scene is one of desolation. The french windows at which* HELEN *was standing are missing, as is the wall, as is* HELEN. *There is a heap of masonry in their place, past which is a fine view over the garden.* SANDRA *is crying quietly;* DAPHNE *is nowhere to be seen*]

His name was Partridge and he lived at Palmer's Green. His widow was a charming lady.

[WANDSWORTH TEETER *appears, picking his way through what were the french windows*]

And of great fortitude. Well, well, she said, as long as he was not blown up in vain, all is for the best. Blown up in vain! I said. Dear lady, we captured a hundred yards of trench.

TEETER [*declaiming*]: My soul was stricken with a great guilt!
CARBOY: It is at times like these that the mettle shows. To be British is everything.
TEETER: Where is Helen?
CARBOY [*looking round*]: Gone to ground, gone to ground . . .
TEETER: There was a cry. Who needs me?

[SANDRA *sobs*]

She?

CARBOY: Learn your place, my girl!
TEETER: Hush. She is ignorant. One must be tolerant.
CARBOY: Half Irish. It's no good . . .
TEETER: Come here, my child.

[SANDRA *goes up to him, head bowed, crying*]

Sit at my feet.

[*She does so*]

What is troubling you?

[*She cries quietly*]

CARBOY: Speak up, my girl!
TEETER: Tolerance, tolerance . . . Look at me, child.

[*She looks up at him*]

Open your heart.
SANDRA: Is it . . . ?
TEETER: What, child?
SANDRA: The end, sir?
CARBOY: Nonsense, nonsense.
TEETER: Hush . . . One moment . . . [*He picks his way through what were the french windows, plucks a blade of grass, and returns. He hands it to* SANDRA]
SANDRA: A blade of grass?
TEETER: Look out there.

[*She does so*]

Do you see where I picked it?
SANDRA: No, sir.
TEETER: How many blades are left?
SANDRA: I don't know, sir.
TEETER: Count them.
SANDRA: I can't, sir.
TEETER: Why not?
SANDRA: There are too many, sir.

TEETER: Shall I put this blade back to fill up the space?

SANDRA: No, sir.

TEETER: Why not?

SANDRA: It doesn't notice, sir.

TEETER: Very good.

SANDRA: But what about the thrushes, sir?

TEETER: It works with thrushes, too.

SANDRA: Oh.

TEETER: Do you understand?

SANDRA: No, sir.

CARBOY: I tell you it's no good.

TEETER: Hush. Listen, my child. What is the relationship between this blade of grass in your hand, and that lawn?

SANDRA: Relationship?

TEETER: Suppose I make this blade of grass disappear. What will happen to the lawn?

SANDRA: Nothing, sir.

TEETER: Suppose I make the lawn disappear. What will happen to this blade of grass?

SANDRA: Nothing, sir.

TEETER: Suppose I make the whole of the lawn disappear but one growing blade of grass. What will happen to that blade?

SANDRA: Sir?

TEETER: Will it grow more, or less, or the same as before?

CARBOY: More. It'll have more space. Unless the moles get it.

[TEETER *sighs*]

That is, if moles eat grass.

SANDRA: It's too complex, sir.

TEETER: All is for the best, my child. All is as it should be. To be otherwise is impossible. Do you understand?

SANDRA: Thrushes, squirrels . . .

TEETER: Thrushes, squirrels, grass, trees. All must pass. We too, we too. What else would you have?

[SANDRA *is puzzled*]

CARBOY: You're wasting your time.

TEETER: Consider a growing flower . . .

[DAPHNE *comes in, with a tray of cups*]

DAPHNE: Cocoa, for all.

CARBOY: Ah, you see?

DAPHNE: The last we'll get from *that* kitchen. [*She hands cocoa to* CARBOY] And where Helen's to sleep tonight I can't imagine. [*She hands cocoa to* SANDRA] However, it'll probably solve itself . . . Wandsworth, how nice to see you again. And I seem to have one cup over.

TEETER [*taking it*]: There is a providence, you see . . .

DAPHNE: I think it may be a hot summer. If only the sun keeps going . . .

[*They sip their cocoa appreciatively, except for* SANDRA *who still sits dazed*]

CARBOY: Ah . . . it's the little things in life which make all the difference.

TEETER: No, no, it's the flow. It's the flow which matters. The *flow*. If we can keep going, if we can just keep going . . .

DAPHNE: For long enough.

CARBOY: Why not? We've got this far. [*He stretches out his arms, and looks down at his feet. He laughs*] Look! No hands!

TEETER: Exactly. Drink your cocoa, my child [*as* SANDRA *sobs*]

DAPHNE: Drink it up, Sandra.

CARBOY: Drink it up, my girl!

[*She does so*]

And be thankful.

CURTAIN

Out of the Flying Pan

by

DAVID CAMPTON

First produced on 4 August 1960 at the Library
Theatre, Scarborough, for Theatre-in-the-Round.
Producer, Stephen Joseph

Cast

A—A DIPLOMAT
B—A DIPLOMAT

Out of the Flying Pan

PLACE: Not far from here.
TIME: Not far from now.

The setting consists of two chairs, one on either side of the stage. Lights come up on a solitary man with a despatch-case. He is waiting. There comes the sound of an approaching aircraft. He becomes attentive. The aircraft passes. He lapses again into time-passing. The sound of an aircraft approaching comes again. He takes no notice. The aircraft lands. He collects himself hurriedly, and looks in all directions at once. An identically dressed man with despatch-case hurries on. They shake hands.

A: How?
B: Nice.
A: Pleasant?
B: Comfortable.
A: Jolly.
B: Time?
A: Exactly.
B: Welcome?
A: Ready.
B: Press?
A: Films.
B: Radio?
A: T.V.
B: Ready?
A: Go.

[*A band plays the opening music of a film newsreel. The two men assume exaggerated postures of greeting. Two different photographs are taken—the first photograph is a handshake, the second photograph is some sign—a clenched fist, 'V' sign, handshake over head, etc.*

The band stops. A steps forward]

A: Freedom and Democracy.

[B *steps forward*]

B: Peace and Friendship.

[A *steps back, and indicates to B that the floor is his. B clears his throat. There is desultory clapping*]

Come Reds. Greeting from the Republic of Republic of Republic of.

[*A roll on the drums as though the National Anthem were about to be played.*

B *springs to attention and takes his hat off.*

A, *who had expected to sit back and take no notice, is caught napping. He springs hastily to attention, and removes his hat. The drum roll ends. B relaxes and puts his hat on again. A follows suit*]

B [*orating*]: This is a hysterical evasion. I come daring the olive. Branch. Our signatures on the Charter will ensure that between our two hate stations will be established a bite of peas, to be enjoyed by our childrens, and our childrens and our childrens—and our childrens. My country devours nothing but peas, will never devour anything but peas, has never devoured anything but peas. Success crown our forts. Piece of Fiendship.

[*He steps back to the sound of applause. He indicates to A that the floor is his. A steps forward, and clears his throat*]

146

A: Yorick's clemency, labels of gender . . . When, on behalf of his Government . . .

[*He takes off his hat, and stands to attention. Nothing happens*]

His Government . . .

[*Still nothing*]

A [*shouting*]: His Government!

[*A single crash on the cymbals.*
A stands easy, and replaces his hat. B waits for something else to happen, but it doesn't]

On behalf of his Government I will gum the reprehensitive of the Republic of Republic of. This is an oars splashing occasion, and I feel that I am hardly guilty of exaggeration if I state that upon the outcome. Our negotiations resist the future of the fee peoples in a whirl.

[*Clapping. B assumes the speech is over, but is disappointed*]

Today we prove the tooth of the old saw 'The Gun is Mightier than the Word'. Today we march beast forward to claim our girl—university hypocrisy. Today we strike a vital blow for the wasted word.

[*Clapping*]

His Garbagemen, and I, your selected preventative, are constipant today will be the girth of a new hero in the history of landslide—well, and hapless of behind.

[*Clapping*]

Three ton of Mockery.

[*He makes a 'V' sign. Clapping.*
The newsreel music is played again. They shake hands. The music ends]

B: Over?
A: Done.
B: Business?
A: Business.

> [A *and* B *each bring a chair into the centre of the stage, and sit facing each other*]

A: Chairman?
B: Chairman.

> [A *stands up*]

A: Open.

> [*He smiles at* B, *and sits again. They smile at each other, and take sheafs of documents from their despatch-cases. Frowning, they hand documents to each other*]

Section A, paragraph B.
B: Sentence Y, Segment C.
A: Portion U.
B: Caution D.
A: One for you.
B: Another for me.
A: Afterthought I.
B: Compromise E.
A: Page in Code.
B: Here's the key.
A: Postscript W.
B: Exhibit G.
A: A two-hour session, and we break for tea.
B: Clause P.
A: Memo three.
B: Division two.
A: Revision V.
B: B.
A: C.

B: D.

A: E.

B: G.

A: P.

B: Tea.

A ⎱ I.T.V.
B ⎰ B.B.C.

[*Each now has the other's pile of papers. They stuff them into their despatch-cases again*]

A: Yes?

B: Yes.

A: Then nothing remains to disturb our complete agreement, and without further ado I shall produce the Treaty.

B: Since nothing remains to disrobe our complete greedment, without further ago you may produce the treat. He.

A: The Charter.

B: The Barter.

A: The Carter.

B: The Garter.

A: Legato.

B: Regatta.

[*A produces an ornate document with seals dangling*]

B: Check?

A: Check.

[*A reads one side of the Charter, hands it to B, who reads the other side. They pass it from one to the other until they have finished reading*]

A: One.

B: Three.

A: Five.

B: Seven.

A: Nine.

B: Ten.
A: Jack.
B: Queen.
A: King.
B: Ace!

[*They shake hands, and take out fountain pens*]

A: Sign?
B: Sign.
A [*orating*]: Never before in the mist re-exhume an affair has such a purple and a staining been achieved between beefsteaks. We underhand the other, and will truss the other illicitly. In the words of our Pride Mister—'Onwards. Forwards. Upwards. Backwards. Sideways.' Three ton of mockery. I thank you.

[*Small fanfare*]

B [*orating*]: I sten here to dodocate my prince of pills. Break down trade. Barriers! I have a way with restrictive practices. No more Eno comic suctions. The Words of the Resident of the Republic of Republic of Republic of. 'Mightier still and mighty shall out of bounds increase. We dance tethered towards a wetter state of things. We can fake it.' Peace of fiendship. I thank you.

[*Small fanfare.*
A bends down to sign, but straightens again, and stares indignantly at B. B shrugs his shoulders, and bends down to sign, but straightens again, and indignantly stares at A]

B: Peace and Friendship.
A: Freedom and Democracy.
B: Gross misrepresentation.
A: Foul misinterpretation.
B: Undiplomatic double-talking.
A: Unconstitutional masquerading.

B: Swiddle.
A: Dindle.
B: Our?
A: Your.
B: Sign?
A: Sign?
B: No.
A: No.

[*They repeat 'no' after each other at a fantastic rate.
B stalks away. He stands in a corner muttering to himself. A
recovers his composure, and goes over to B. He straightens
his tie, and clears his throat*]

A: Tup of twee?

[*There is no reply*]

Tup of twee?
B [*growling*]: Tup of twee!
A [*enthusiastically*]: Tup of twee.
B [*scornfully*]: Tup of twee!
A [*coaxing*]: Tup of twee.
B [*slightly melting*]: Tup of twee?
A [*That's it, old man!*]: Tup of twee!
B [*graciously accepting*]: Tup of twee.

[*They return to their seats, where A pours out tea. B accepts*]

A: Nice?
B: Nice.

[*They drink*]

A [*chattily*]: Last year our exports included tons of assorted
phosphates, an enormous quantity of canned partridges,
a large amount of cokernut confectionery, six out-of-date
aircraft, five brass door-knobs, four ladies-in-waiting,

three blind mice, two Chelsea Pensioners, and something in a pear tree.

B [*chattily*]: Last year our population included Slavs, Slaves, Slobs, Nobs, Hobs, Whitejackets, Blackjackets, Leatherjackets, and Jailbirds.

A: Our rainfall is the envy of civilized society, and we have mountain ranges which could hardly be manufactured elsewhere in the world.

B: Our building programme includes ice houses, boiler houses, light houses, dark houses, power houses, and sand castles.

A: Friendly?

B: Friendly.

A: Handshake?

B: Hand brake.

> [*They shake hands. They turn away emotionally, and wipe their eyes, taking off their spectacles to do so. They turn back again and shake hands, and pat each other on the back. The spectacles get exchanged. When they put them on again, they are both as blind as bats. They grope around until they find one another. They exchange spectacles again, laugh, and shake hands again*]

A: We resume.

B: Assume.

A: Presume.

B: Exhume.

A: The Charter?

B: The Charter.

A: The Charter provides in each case for substantial disarmament.

B: Ban of the comic bomb.

A: Disestablishment of frontier gods.

B: In sport of which, maps of the area in question shall be affixed to the Charter.

[They rummage in their despatch-cases, and each produces a map]

A: The territory administered by His Grudgement.
B: The Republic of Republic of Republic of.
A: The far-flung Umpire.
B: The Republic of Republic of Republic of.
A: The Common on which the sun never sits.
B: The Republic of Republic of Republic of.
A: The Family of Stations.
B: The . . . *[He decides not to]*

[Each examines the other's map. At first they make routine inspections, then each notices something wrong with the map he is holding. They sidle together, and look over one another's maps]

A: Fundamental error.
B: Ridiculous mistake.
A: The Government Strip.
B: The Republican Strait.
A: Ours.
B: Ours.
A: The Government Strip contains valuable mineral deposits, rich farm lands, thriving factories, and a contented population. His Government considers the Strip necessary to its economic security and balance of payments.
B: The Republican Strait consists of a canal vital to the free passage of shipping, and the protection of inland ports. The Republic has a duty to ensure the security of world shipping.
A: The Strip consists merely of uncultivated bushland and arid stone crops. The natives are wild and unco-operative.
B: The Strait consists only of unnavigable waterways, and undrained swamps. Surveyors pronounce it useless.
A: Nevertheless the principle must be upheld.
B: Nevertheless aggression must be repelled.

A: The honour of His Government has been doubted.

B: The dignity of the Republic has been flouted.

A: Notes will be passed.

B: Protests will be noted.

A: Questions will be asked.

B: Precedents quoted.

A: This means . . .

B: This means . . .

A: Armed combat.

B: Submarines.

A: Horse Marines.

B: Forces ready to march. Soldiers.

A: Guns.

B: Aircraft.

A: Germs.

B: Secret weapons.

A: Secret service.

B: Rockets.

A: Bombs.

B: Exasperation.

A: Desperation.

B: Devastation.

A: Annihilation.

[*They bristle at each other, then turn their backs on each other. After a minute, B begins to feel that the position is slightly ridiculous. He peeps back at A. A is stiff and unrelenting. B makes an effort, turns round, and addresses A's back*]

B: Grasping swine.

[A *stiffens even harder*]

[*Coaxing*] Grasping swine?

[*He makes a noise like a cork coming out of a bottle*]

Grasping swine.

A [*light dawning*]: Grasping swine!
B: Grasping swine.

> [A *turns to him.* B *pours out two glasses of wine. He hands one to* A. *They raise their glasses*]

A: Proast.
B: Proast.

> [*They drink*]

A: His Government seeks only full employment, and fiscal stability.
B: Furtive grasp?
A: Furtive grasp.

> [B *pours out two further glasses*]

Mud.
B: Mud.

> [*They drink*]

A: His Giverment wishes only to assist world enterprise, free markets, and jolly good fellows.
B: Underpast?
A: Under past.

> [B *pours out another two glasses*]

Wizzle.
B: Wizzle.

> [*They drink*]

A: His Gushment insists on shaking hands all round.

> [*They shake hands*]

In spite of past misunderstanding, I feel confident in the generous interpretation of Government policy—in the— er—interpretation of generous Government policy—in

the—er—policy of general Government interpretation—
er . . .

B: Granted.

A: We believe in moral responsibilities, in self-government,
and democratic constitutions, improved living conditions,
stubborn resistance to defeatism, and resolute pursuit of
sound policies.

B: We renounce the use of violence for political ends,
flagrant violation of international law, states of emergency,
and expansionist activities.

A: Unconditional withdrawal?

B: Non-belligerence.

A: Free navigation.

B: General assurance.

A: Peace with honour.

B: Long endurance.

    [*They embrace*]

A: Proof.

B: Proof.

A [*handing over a bunch of papers*]: Take them.

B [*handing over a bunch of papers*]: Take them.

    [*They hand over papers to each other*]

A: Mandates.

B: Protectorates.

A: Satellites.

B: Stations.

A: Colonies.

B: Dependencies.

A: Commonwealth.

B: Nations.

A [*handing over his map*]: The Government Strip.

B [*handing over his map*]: The Republican Strait.

A: Agreed?

B: Agreed.
A: Sign?
B: Sign.

> [*They take out their fountain pens again.*
> *A signs. B signs.*
> *They shake hands. Newsreel music. They pose. Newsreel*
> *music ends. Without looking at each other again, they pick*
> *up their newly acquired maps, and gloat over them, back to*
> *back*]

B: The Government Strip.
A: The Republican Strait.

> [*A thought strikes simultaneously through their joys. They*
> *sober. They glance behind at each other*]

A [*hugging map*]: Our.
B [*hugging map*]: Our.
A: We.
B: To me from you.
A: From you to me.
B: Trick!
A: Trap!
B: Blind.
A: Bait.
B [*tearing map in half*]: Renounce.
A [*tearing map in half*]: Pronounce.
B: Announce.
A: Denounce.
B: The Charter.
A: The Grafter.
B: Perverter.
A: Deserter.

> [*B tears the Charter in half.*
> *A tears the halves in half.*

B *tears half the remainder.*
A *tears half the remainder*]

A: Cease?
B: Peace?
A: Never. [*Tears one of his documents in half*]
B: No. [*Tears one of his documents in half*]

[*They repeat 'no' after each other with fantastic rapidity. As they do so, they tear up documents. They toss the torn paper about until the air is filled with fluttering pieces. Amplified 'no's' give way to sounds of war—guns and sirens. A picks up his chair, and carries it to one side of the stage. B picks up his chair, and carries it to the other side of the stage. As they speak, A and B mime various acts of war—flying planes, dropping bombs, dive-bombing, etc; all with the glee of schoolboys enjoying a game*]

A: One air squadron wiped out.
B: One city exterminated.
A: Two divisions lost.
B: Two islands annihilated.
A: Navy gone.
B: Transport dislocated.
A: Ten million citizens dead.
B: Population eradicated.

[*The sounds of war are amplified to a climax. As A and B cease to speak, there comes the roar of a cosmic-sized explosion*]

A: Nothing left.
B: Nothing left.

[B *leaves the stage.*
Silence for a few seconds. A bird twitters.
Music. Gentle classical-ballet-type music. A *does a little semi-ballet, picking up the torn paper, and putting it in his*

brief-case. The music ends and A *stands in the middle of the stage.*

There comes the sound of an approaching aircraft. He becomes attentive. The aircraft passes. He lapses again into time-passing. The sound of an aircraft comes again. It lands. B *hurries on. They shake hands*]

A: How?
B: Nice.
A: Pleasant?
B: Comfortable.
A: Jolly.
B: Time?
A: Exactly.
B: Welcome?
A: Ready.
B: Press?
A: Films.
B: Radio?
A: T.V.
B: Ready?
A: Go.

BLACKOUT